# Walk Around the World

# Walk Around the World

Healings, Miracles, Power
Encounters and Other
First-Person Accounts from
Earth's Frontiers

Compiled by
Marilynne E. Foster

Christian Publications
CAMP HILL, PENNSYLVANIA

*This book is dedicated to*

## Helen Mae Powell Constance

*woman of God*
*wife, mother, missionary*
*and author,*
*who took her final step of faith*
*into the arms of her Savior,*
*July 12, 1995.*

Christian Publications
3825 Hartzdale Drive, Camp Hill, PA 17011

*Faithful, biblical publishing since 1883*

ISBN: 0-87509-639-5
LOC Catalog Card Number: 95-83955
© 1996 by Christian Publications, Inc.
All rights reserved
Printed in the United States of America

96  97  98  99  00     5  4  3  2  1

# CONTENTS

1   Dear Little Thief ............................. 1

2   Jesus Lives in This Village ....................... 7

3   God's Angels................................ 11

4   Star ................................ 15

5   Stop Praying................................ 19

6   Don't Feel Sorry for Us! ........................ 23

7   The Saga of the Kpelé Translation........ 29

8   Breakdown in Saldou............................ 33

9   Romance, Missionary Style ..................... 37

10  Cannibal Valley................................ 41

11  Carjacked at Gunpoint .......................... 47

12  Prisoners of the Lord ......................... 53

13  Chanta's Prayer................................ 57

14  A Little Pain—A Lot of Gain.................. 61

15  A Dyak Stands Up for Jesus.................. 65

16  Dear Mom and Dad .............................. 69

17  God Stops the Fire................................ 75

18  God's Miracle................................ 79

19  A Girl Like Esther ................................ 83

20  Mama Christine ...................................... 89

21  "Are You Healed?" ................................. 93

22  The Incredible Journey ........................... 95

23  The Hiding Place .................................. 101

24  Healed! ................................................. 107

25  The High God's Hippos ....................... 111

26  God Is the Healer ................................. 117

27  I Can? ................................................. 121

28  God's Mule ......................................... 127

29  A Crib and a Shaker ............................ 129

30  The Right People in the Right Places ... 133

31  My Turn .............................................. 137

32  We'll Be Back ..................................... 145

33  Adios! ................................................. 151

# DEAR LITTLE THIEF

## COLOMBIA, SOUTH AMERICA

### Helen Constance

S treet children in Colombia and in many other parts of the world have become famous for their ability to survive. They sleep on the street, steal food from open markets and, when caught, are beaten without mercy by merchants who hate them.

Mothers, abandoned by their men after having numerous children, in desperation often force four- or five-year-olds to scrounge for themselves. Those children accept their situation as normal and, after years of such living, can no longer tolerate the restriction of an organized life.

One day our son Joey was playing in front of our house with a set of toy pistols and a belt and holster. Suddenly, an eight-year-old jumped him, beat him on the head and ripped off the belt and guns.

Joey, bruised and crying, came running in to tell me about it. I grabbed my keys and took off after the little thief as he ran up one street and down another. I was determined to get those guns! American toys were very expensive in Colombia.

The boy ran through buildings and across yards but I always caught up with him as he crossed

1

streets. As we approached a building under construction, the boy cut across the property.

"Catch that thief!" I called to some workers.

To my amazement, the men dropped their tools and took off after the little culprit and caught him. Soon they brought the panting boy to me. What did I want to do with him, they wondered aloud.

Just then a police car came by and the men told my story. I asked that the boy be released since I now had the toy guns. But the policeman insisted on taking the boy to the police station. The boy, he said, needed to understand that the law had been broken and he should be punished.

I followed the police car to the station. The boy's name, I learned, was Vicente. The officer in charge ruffed him up a bit, bawled him out and then asked what I wanted them to do with him. I knew that having a bed in jail would be no punishment for one who was used to sleeping on sidewalks. Anyway, one night in jail would not change him.

I took a long look at the child. His eyes locked with mine, defying me to punish him. I felt pity for him. He had never had shoes, much less a toy gun. Before I knew it, I heard myself telling the officer that I would take him home with me. As we headed to the car I made sure to maintain a firm grip on his hand. I didn't want to lose him now.

Back at the house, I gave him soap and told him to shower. After a few minutes he emerged looking the same as when he went in. I ordered him back to the shower with instructions on how to lather his body. Soon he looked like the Abominable Snowman. He combed through the lather with a fine-tooth comb to get out the head lice. After three lathers and combings, I left him rinsing while I looked through Joey's clothes and picked out a few. With his skin shiny clean, hair combed and dressed in fresh clothes, Vicente looked downright handsome. I was proud of him.

When a meal was set before him, he stared in amazement, self-conscious about using a fork. He was used to grabbing his food on the run. And it was news to him that he should thank God for it.

On Sunday, when we took him to church, we wondered if he would bolt down the street. But he sat, groomed and interested. Each day we had family devotions and he began to learn Scripture. We explained the gospel to him and after three weeks he prayed and gave his heart to Christ.

One day a lady graduate from our Bible institute was passing through Cali on her way to teach in a small boarding school in the mountains. The teacher suggested that Vicente go with her to the school. We were anxious that he be educated, so we packed his things and paid the fees.

As he was leaving, Vicente ran back to the house.

"I forgot my toothbrush!" he grinned. Brushing teeth was a new experience for him. I hugged the little transformed thief we had come to love. It seemed that we were sending another son off to experience the joy of education. We rejoiced by faith at what God would do in his life.

Then, suddenly, the violence of the civil war invaded that part of the country. Word came that everyone had fled from the mountains. No one could give us information about the teacher, the Christian families or students. But according to the news, many people had been killed.

We never heard from Vicente again. But we knew one thing—he knew how to run! We hoped he had escaped into the hills.

There are millions of children like Vicente in the world who will never lie in a clean bed or bow their heads in prayer. It would be wonderful to end this story with Vicente as a leader in a church somewhere in Colombia. Perhaps he is.

The street children of Colombia have become so numerous and their thievery so bold that people have begun shooting them. The kids have taken shelter in the huge dark and filthy tunnels beneath the city where sewage runs. I cannot help but wonder who would be willing to go as a missionary to the children of the sewers?

The Vicentes of Colombia cry out for help.

> Dear little thief
>   You make me feel sad;
> You steal and you swear
>   But you're not really bad.
>
> You run like a deer
>   After stealing a bread
> And knock people down and
>   Don't care if they're dead.
>
> You lie and you cheat,
>   You curse and connive,
> But I know you do it
>   To just stay alive.
>
> The merchants will beat you
>   When you steal their fruit,
> But they seldom can catch you
>   With your bag of loot.

Some days you are hungry
 When stealing goes bad;
It's feast or it's famine—
 Your life is so sad!

No place to go home to,
 No mother to care
That your clothes are ragged
 And there's lice in your hair.

When you have a fever
 A stairwell's the spot
To curl up and suffer
 And ponder your lot.

Although you are eight
 You still cannot read;
All you can manage
 Is your stomach's need.

At night in the shadows
 With no pillow or sheet
In the dangerous city
 You sleep on concrete.

Sometimes when the moonlight
 Shines on your face
You look like an angel,
 An angel displaced.

Down on the corner
 There's a church you pass by
Where you can take refuge
 When you want to cry.

Dear little beggar-boy,
 Please go in there;
They'll tell you of Jesus
 And offer a prayer.

The Lord died to save you
   And offers His love;
He's prepared you a home
   In heaven above.

Dear, dear little thief
   Whom I cannot forget;
Your smile breaks my heart
   And my pillow is wet.

There's so many of you
   On streets everywhere—
Slum children so needy
   Of our love and our prayer.

May the God of compassion
   Make us willing to give
That you, little thief,
   May eternally live.

May He help us remember
   Your tears and distress
When the food on our tables
   We ask Him to bless.

*"And whoever welcomes a little child
like this in my name welcomes me."*
Matthew 18:5

# JESUS LIVES IN THIS VILLAGE

## THAILAND, SOUTHEAST ASIA ———

### Neal C. Webber

The incidence of leprosy in northeast Thailand was, in 1957, the second highest in the world. After just a few years there were more than 1,200 names on the rolls of three mission treatment centers where people came every two weeks to receive medicine. Within months we had our first convert, and then another and another.

At one center, called Nong Bua Laai, there was a group of new believers who every Friday walked in 10 miles from their village. They'd sleep overnight in the grass-roofed shelter to await the medicine distribution the following morning. One day the group asked if I would be willing to come to their village and dedicate a small chapel if they would build it. I was thrilled and a little amazed at their request, but agreed to do it.

About a month later they told me that the chapel was completed. I promised to come the following week.

The first part of the journey was by train, followed by a 10-mile walk. Finally I came within sight of the village. A neat little grass chapel perched at the perimeter.

It had been a long, tiresome trek. I went in, sat

down on a bench across the front of the room and took a big drink from my thermos. My ears perked up as I heard a large truck approaching. *I sure wish I had known there was a truck coming here. I'd have much rather had a ride,* I muttered to myself.

I watched the truck approach the village and turn in the direction of the chapel. The driver turned off the engine, got out and walked up to where I was sitting. Putting his hands together in the customary Thai greeting, he said, "Hello, Adjahn. You are the missionary who has been telling the Christians in this village about Jesus, aren't you?"

I returned his greeting and answered him affirmatively.

"I'm glad to meet you," he replied. "I'd like to tell you that I know that Jesus lives in this village."

I was startled.

"Oh, are you a Christian? Are you part of the group that built this chapel?" I asked him.

"Oh, no," the trucker replied. "I'm not a Christian but I know that Jesus lives in this village!"

He turned and pointed to a nearby house.

"Last week," he continued, "I drove into the village to pick up rice for the mill. I noticed a large crowd of people around that house so I stopped the truck and walked over to see what was going on. A young boy, about 10 years old, was lying on the porch. His foot was badly cut. The blood was pouring from it.

"The people told me that that morning the boy had picked up his huge bolo knife to cut some bamboo shoots to be used for the family's curry pot. He found a clump of bamboo that he thought was just right to cut. He took a big swing, but evidently his knife hit a piece of dry bamboo. Instead of cutting in, the knife glanced off and nearly severed two toes and the tip of a third. He was bleeding badly. Some thought he might bleed to death."

The truck driver continued. "Some neighbors were very concerned and began to tie some spirit strings around the boy's wrists and ankles and neck. Someone even tied a spirit string around the whole house. That way, they believe, the spirits would be prevented from taking the boy's spirit away.

"Then someone remembered that the village Christians always talked about how great Jesus is and how He can help the sick and do great things. 'Maybe we should ask the Christians to come and pray,' someone suggested.

"While I was watching all of this, they brought two Christian young men about 18 years old to see the boy. Someone finally asked them if they would pray and ask Jesus to stop the bleeding. The youths said, 'No. If Jesus stops the bleeding, all of you will say that it was the spirits that stopped the blood. If you'll take off the spirit strings, we will pray.'

"Well, even as they said this, the boy himself pulled the strings off his wrists. Someone else took the ones off his ankles and neck and someone else tore down the one around the house.

"Now," the truck driver continued, "I don't know why the Christians close their eyes when they talk to Jesus, but I didn't close mine. I was no more than three feet away from the foot that had blood spurting out of it. When the young man who was praying asked Jesus to please stop the bleeding, right there in front of my eyes I saw a big drop of blood form and the blood stopped flowing. I was so amazed I got goose bumps all over—I saw Jesus stop the bleeding. I knew He had to be there. I looked all around but I could not see Him. Everybody was surprised and very happy. So, Adjahn, that is how I know that Jesus lives in this village."

I was surprised and amazed, too, that a non-Christian was telling me this story with such sincerity.

"Have you ever heard the story about Jesus and how He is able to change people's lives?" I asked. "Have the Christians ever talked with you about becoming a Christian?"

"Oh, yes, Adjahn! I have talked with them and in my heart I know that I should be a Christian. And do you know what? I have made up my mind that I will become one. And when I become a Christian I want to be a real one—just like the Christians here."

The man went on to explain that he was doing some things that he knew were wrong but that he liked doing. He believed he could no longer do them if he became a Christian. I tried to convince him that now was the time to receive Christ, while he had the opportunity. But he drove off, assuring me that he would do it some day soon.

Some months later I asked about the truck driver. One of the Christians told me that just the week before, the man had been eating noodles at the market in a nearby town. Someone put poison in the soup and he died. Had he given his heart to Christ?

I could only hope so.

> *"I tell you, now is the time of God's favor,*
> *now is the day of salvation."*
> 2 Corinthians 6:2

# GOD'S ANGELS

## Elizabeth Abrams

It was the early 1970s. A rebel branch of the Maguindanao Muslims was beginning to war against the Philippine government. Their aim was to make the whole island of Mindanao a separate Muslim country.

Our son Philip, then a teenager, was attending the local high school in the town of Cotabato. One day, he asked if he could invite his friend Juan to stay overnight. Philip thought it would be an opportunity for Juan to see what a Christian home was like.

After supper that night, my husband Jay said, "Let's have our evening devotions." Philip thought to himself, *How will Juan feel about our reading the Bible? He goes to the local Catholic church, but I am sure he knows nothing about the Bible.*

My husband read Psalm 91 including the verses about God sending His angels to watch over people. Noting that the passage used the word angels in its plural form, he said, "This means there must be at least two angels guarding each person. Since there are eight of us in this house [a Filipino family lived with us], there must be at least 16 angels here right now."

Before half an hour had passed, shots rang out and we heard a loud rumble out on our dead-end street. Quickly we turned the lights off.

The rumble stopped in front of our house. It was a military tank preparing to set up a command base at the end of the street. As we sat in the dark listening to the soldiers in the tank talk to their counterparts out in the field, our thoughts were centered on those angels. *I sure hope they are around here right now!* Philip thought. *Were they protecting us?* I wondered. God's Word had promised that they would.

We listened as our Chinese neighbor, who ran a chicken farm nearby, arrived in his truck and took his family to safety. The soldiers yelled at him for not staying in the security of his home.

"We could have shot at you," they kept yelling. At that point we realized that our angels had done at least one thing so far—they had kept us in our house even when a friend had phoned to invite us to come to the safety of his cement-walled room a mile away.

The next day we learned that the soldiers had burned all the Muslim homes in the surrounding fields "just in case they were harboring rebel forces."

This was the beginning of three years of a regional guerrilla war during which we daily experienced the miraculous protection of God and His angels.

Night after night rebels shot in our direction. A morning inspection of our home often revealed a roof full of shrapnel. Ours was the only two-story home in this sparsely settled area, an obvious and visible target. For safety's sake, at night we slept on the bare floor in a downstairs room. Artillery often blasted through the night silence all around us. Dawn found us venturing upstairs to wash and change clothes and work at the desk in our office, trying to keep our life as normal as possible.

One day, as I sat at my typewriter next to my husband at his, something came flying through the screened window, zipped past my neck and hit the wall.

"What was that?" I asked Jay.

"That's a bullet," he said, picking up the object at my feet. Apparently someone had shot at a military spotter plane flying overhead. Failing to hit its target, the bullet had gone wild, slicing through our bedroom window.

There were other "victims" of war on our property. Rain tanks are a major component of missionary life. We had two large ones on a platform in our yard. One Saturday morning a shot put a hole in the bottom of one of the tanks. All the carefully collected water ran out. The very next week, another bullet hit the other tank, again, right in the bottom.

Travel, too, was perilous. When we rode the local jeeps into town, people would ask, "Why don't you go to Manila like the rich people in town?" Our answer was, "God brought us to this province. It has been our home for 20 years and until God tells us differently, we are here to stay." Later we learned that the military had investigated our influence in the area and decided it was best to leave us there because our presence had a calming effect on the local populace.

Do we believe in angels? Most certainly. We believe the Lord, the Most High of Psalm 91, still commands His angels to guard those who make Him their dwelling place and refuge.

> *"If you make the Most High your dwelling—even the*
> *Lord, who is my refuge—then no harm will*
> *befall you, no disaster will come near your tent.*
> *For he will command his angels concerning you*
> *to guard you in all your ways."*
> Psalm 91:9-11

# STAR

## PERU, South America

### Faith E. Scarrow

The ladies were leaving my home one morning after a Bible study when Estrella (Star), a neighbor, walked by and noticed the women filing out the front door.

"What is going on?" she wondered aloud. I explained that we were having a weekly Bible study. She said she would love to come but was involved with another course held at the same time. I assured her that when she finished that course she was welcome to attend. That was in November.

December 25 is always a special day at our Mission house in Lima, Peru. Our whole missionary team gathers there to share dinner and a time of fellowship and games. That particular Christmas day we were about to eat when the doorbell rang. It was my neighbor, Estrella.

She reported that her only son George, 13 years old, had been involved in an accident. She wanted me to pray as she traveled to where the accident had occurred. The only thing she knew about me at that point was that the neighborhood children called me "Señora Madre" (Mrs. Mother) and I was a "religious" person. We agreed to pray for George.

15

Later that evening, as we were getting ready for bed, the doorbell rang. A neighbor lady asked me to come quickly. She told me that George had been shot in the head and that Estrella was calling for me. Evidently some teenaged boys were playing with guns and one went off. George had received a bullet in the temple.

Estrella's house was full of family and friends. George was there, too, laid out in a coffin in the middle of the living room. The parish priest was there, along with several nuns. One nun was Estrella's aunt. She separated herself from the group and led me upstairs to where another large group of people were gathered.

I found Estrella kneeling in the middle of the room, banging her head on the floor and screaming "God help me!" in a loud voice.

"Oh Lord, help me to glorify You," I prayed as I approached the weeping woman.

I got down on my knees beside Estrella. "I'm here," I whispered in her ear. I took her in my arms.

"Faith, please do something," she cried. "I can't stand the pain in my heart. It's going to kill me."

I began to sing "Alleluia" and followed with other songs of praise one after another. As I sang, a strange thing happened—a calmness spread over the room. There was peace.

When I stopped singing, Estrella asked me to continue. So began the longest impromptu concert of my life. Once I had sung all the songs I could remember in Spanish, I began in English. No one seemed to mind. I was still singing two-and-a-half hours later when Estrella finally fell asleep on her bed.

The next day, my husband Don and I attended the funeral service in her home. I believe George went to be with the Lord. He had attended a vacation Bible school at the Mission the previous summer and had given his heart to Christ.

In the days and weeks that followed, Estrella and I became friends. I would often go to her home to counsel and console her. Seeing her suffer so deeply made me desperate to lead her to the Lord since I knew that He was the One who could heal the brokenhearted.

Eventually I found out that Estrella was a pharmacist and her husband was a medical doctor. They had been separated for many years and she had been left with the home and their only son. She came from a well-known family. She also had an uncle who was a minister in the government.

One day I baked a cake and decided to take some to Estrella. Imagine my surprise to find her gone! I knocked on the door of the next-door neighbor and asked where Estrella was. Apparently she had been taken to a hospital because she was suicidal.

I went to the hospital and found Estrella in a room with another patient. She was tied to the bed and obviously drugged. At her request, I spoke to the authorities and received permission to take her home with me.

At first Estrella did not want to eat or dress. She just wanted to stay in bed day after day. Little by little, however, with some coaxing and special effort to make the meals attractive, she began to eat. While she ate, I sang to her and read portions of Scripture. And we showered her with the love of Jesus and prayed.

After about a week, Estrella began to ask questions. It wasn't long before she opened her heart to the Lord and accepted Him as her personal Savior.

The days and weeks that followed were difficult as Estrella tried to put her life back together. She went to church with us and continued to attend the Bible studies in our home. When it came time for us to return to North America for furlough, Estrella was devastated. And yet she believed the Lord would direct her future. He did just that.

The neighbors took a collection and gave Estrella enough money to go to the United States to start her life over again. Today Estrella continues to witness to the life-changing power of the Lord Jesus Christ.

*"I have come that they may have life,*
*and have it to the full."*
John 10:10

# STOP PRAYING

## THAILAND, SOUTHEAST ASIA———

### Dorothy Undheim

Looking for the English Bible I had left in one of the 18,000 taxis in Bangkok, a metropolis of 6 million people, was like looking for a needle in a haystack. Although the situation seemed impossible, I comforted myself in the fact that with God anything is possible and pursued the only recourse I knew at the moment—prayer.

I asked various groups and individuals, both Thai and English, to join the prayer search for my missing Bible. It had become a very close friend and somewhat of a journal after over 10 years of constant usage. It was even more precious because it had been a gift to me by my best friend, my husband Paul, who had died of cancer just a few years before. I was finding the double loss hard to bear.

"Lord," I prayed, "please don't let harm come to my Bible."

I decided to purchase an inexpensive version in the meantime, reminding the Lord that it was "only until You bring back my own to me." But my very words seemed to boomerang as I read the heading of the *Daily Bread* devotional entitled, "Stop Praying." The article went on to say that

God had told Joshua to get up off his knees. "On this occasion something other than prayer was needed," it continued. "We should not ask God to do things we can do for ourselves."

"What do I do, Lord?" I asked.

Phoning the hundreds of taxi companies became discouraging to say the least. So an office girl at the Mission guest house helped me make a large poster to hang in the company offices announcing my loss and offering a 500 peso ($25) reward to anyone who would return the "English book in a black zippered case."

I also took to the streets of Bangkok in search of taxi drivers. Approached at random, most gazed in total amazement at the naive foreigner and answered, "Ma'am, there are hundreds of taxi companies and, furthermore, the taxi with your Bible in it might be privately owned."

Another driver said, "No way. Consider it a lost cause, ma'am. Do you realize the immensity of this city and the number of taxis?"

"Yes," I responded. I knew it all too well.

"Lord, what next?" I prayed in bewilderment.

*Ask for advice,* responded a still small voice in my mind.

Finally, one driver, more patient than the others, listened to my plea.

"Get in, ma'am," he said. "I'll drive you home and give you some advice on the way. All taxi drivers listen to the radio and read the newspaper. Have it announced twice daily at 10 *baht* (50 cents) per day for a week and have it printed in the *Siam Rut* paper (free of charge) which is most widely read by taxi drivers."

"What a good idea," I said enthusiastically. "I

think I'll try that." I thanked the driver for his advice and got out at my doorstep.

The next day I was welcomed warmly at the radio station and proceeded to explain my mission.

"How come you speak Thai?" they wanted to know. "Are you employed by the embassy?" "Why such a large reward for a Bible?" "Couldn't you buy one cheaper than that?" "Aren't they all the same?" Soon a small crowd was gathered around, listening as I explained why this particular Bible was precious to me. I also took the opportunity to tell them that they were precious to God, too, and that He had sent His Son to die for them.

Before I left, I reached into my purse and pulled out some colorful tracts. They accepted them graciously and assured me that, beginning the next morning, the announcement about my missing Bible would be aired twice daily. The newspaper office also promised to print the missing book announcement.

As I walked out the door, I began praying for all who would read and hear the announcement, especially for the taxi driver in whose vehicle the Bible was left.

Some time later a young man appeared at the guest house and handed my Bible to the office girl. As he turned to leave, she asked him for his name and address, mentioning there was a reward being offered for the return of the Bible.

He replied that his taxi driver friend had asked him to bring it and that he himself knew only his friend's street address, but not his house number. I wrote a letter to the address, asking for both the taxi driver and his friend to come and claim the reward. The letter was returned, marked "Insufficient Address."

The day of miracles is not past. But it now appears that I may be on another search—this time for the taxi driver. He needs to know why that Book was so precious to me.

> *"Trust in the LORD with all your heart*
> *and lean not on your own understanding;*
> *in all your ways acknowledge him,*
> *and he will make your paths straight."*
> Proverbs 3:5-6

# DON'T FEEL SORRY FOR US!

## GABON, West Africa

### David Bill

We are David and Teresa Bill, missionaries to Gabon, West Africa. As missionaries, we have been the recipients of sympathy and special attention. But we're not looking for sympathy or special attention. What we, like other missionaries around the world, are looking for are people who will pray for us, for our family, for our needs, for our ministry. Pray for us—but please don't feel sorry for us.

Don't feel sorry for us—we know we are where God wants us!

We wouldn't trade our lives for any others. We like what we do. There is adventure, travel, meeting different people from all over the world. We travel the roads and streets of the city of Port Gentil, then head out off-road to villages by truck, plane or boat.

We lived for eight years on an island with beautiful beaches. Some people pay lots of money to vacation in places like that. In all these places there is a need for the gospel. God has called us to be here and make disciples.

Don't feel sorry for us—we know we are doing what God wants us to do!

We don't want your sympathy because we have been obedient to the call of missions. Teresa did not come from a Christian nor a church-going family as I did. Her home was a broken one, void of Christian values.

"Praise God," Teresa says, "for the precious neighbor lady who invited me to church and faithfully drove me there each week. During my high school years, while I was seeking God's will for my life, the pastor challenged me to become a missionary. That's what I wanted, too!"

Obedience! You can't afford not to be obedient. Obedience is not easy, but you can't afford not to be obedient!

Don't feel sorry for us because we're not in a North American ministry.

In Gabon, we live in a day of unparalleled harvest. Hundreds are turning to Christ from heathenism, from lives once steeped in the fear and superstition of the occult, laden with sin, sickness and disease. Yes, they are turning to Christ by the hundreds.

Ministry here is what we call "generic." Meetings are simple, yet complete. We love it. This doesn't mean there are no problems. In fact, one of the biggest problems is that people seek experiences rather than a relationship with Jesus.

Our ministry is not entertainment geared. We don't need frills, gimmicks, decorations, dinners and the like. We are free of this. Besides, we have a low budget. Simply teaching the Word of God with practical applications is enough. So don't feel sorry for us because we are not in a North American ministry.

Don't feel sorry for us because of our living conditions.

Yes, it's hot and humid in Gabon most of the year. We tolerate it. Yes, we get uncomfortable and not everything is convenient. And we don't like it. But we don't live for comfort or convenience. They are not our gods. Besides, if we get too comfortable we get soft and forget what it means to sacrifice. We're not packing up and leaving because of a few inconveniences.

There are no fast food restaurants. We grind our own hamburger; we mix up milk. We make our own ice cream. Certain foods are not available and if they are, the price is three times the price in the USA. But I ask you, "Have you ever seen an undernourished missionary?"

Don't feel sorry for us because we have left family and friends.

We miss our family and friends but God gives us family and friends among other missionaries. Our annual conference is like one big family reunion. To the children, everyone is aunt and uncle. We also have many friends among the Africans. Often families in the States do not see one another for years. We at least visit our families every five years. If you want to feel sorry for someone, you can feel sorry for the grandparents who get left behind.

Don't feel sorry for us because our children go to boarding school.

We knew when we signed on the dotted line that our children would probably go to boarding school, although sometimes there are other options. We are not cruel, insensitive parents and our children are not weird. We have carefully prepared them for going away to live with an extended family and dorm parents who love and care for them like their own.

The school offers a good private education without the social pressures of the American lifestyle. And besides, our children have had many exciting adventures with us in our ministry, such as river trips to villages and exposure to different cultures. They truly are privileged kids!

Don't feel sorry for us because missionary life is not all that terrific.

We live in a different culture from our own, often among people who don't like foreigners. I don't pretend that the Gabonese are the most loveable people to work with, but I am sure that they say the same about us time-bound North Americans.

We are foreigners. That means "rich," someone to exploit, someone to steal from. There is the constant pressure of the "haves" versus the "have nots." Living in a different culture forces me to see myself in a different light. I am learning a lot about myself. Some things are okay; much is not so good. It's been good to be stretched beyond my comfort zone.

Don't feel sorry for us because we are career missionaries.

We recognize that the Great Commission will

only be fulfilled by spending time in language study and incarnating ourselves for an extended period of time. We are williing to pay the price of investing ourselves long-term to be where God wants us. Short-term missions is good, but it is not the best method for discipling people and building churches.

Don't feel sorry for me because I'm a "poor" missionary.

You've heard the statement that money isn't everything. We told the Lord that we are not looking to earn big money but that we are servants for His kingdom and we want to be satisfied in our work. The Lord meets our needs. Our salaries are adequate and with careful planning and saving we will have a retiral account.

One summer when I was a college student, I was preparing to go on a summer missions trip. My aunt was very upset with me and said, "But you'll be a poor missionary!"

I told her, "Will I lack food, clothing or shelter? No? Then I will have what I need."

Don't feel sorry for us!

Pray for us!

> *"The one who calls you is faithful
> and he will do it."*
> 1 Thessalonians 5:24

# THE SAGA OF THE KPELÉ TRANSLATION

## GUINEA, WEST AFRICA

### Ann McEwen

"In the mid-1930s we, the Kpelé people, invited Christian and Missionary Alliance missionaries to our area deep in the rain forest of Guinea. And soon a Kpelé church was born.

"Our first missionaries recognized the need to get the Word of God translated into the heart-language of the Kpelé believers. Eventually they started translating the Bible, a long and tedious but exciting job.

"Soon our New Testament was nearly completed in typed manuscript form. But the president of Guinea expelled all missionaries except a small remnant. There was no longer anyone here to help us finish the translation. There was no one to pull strings—or whatever one had to do to transform that stack of paper into a book. Nor did the church have the financial where-with-all to publish a book. When the missionaries left, they handed us those cartons of paper with words.

"But what could we do?

"Store them. Maybe the Almighty would one day look on us with favor and send more missionaries to Guinea.

"Someday. Maybe . . ."

29

Guinea is a tropical country. The tropics are noted for cockroaches and termites—big ones—who all thrive on wood and wood products like paper.

A lifetime of effort, the Kpelé New Testament manuscript, was destroyed, eaten! I'm sure Satan was rejoicing over this setback. But God is on the throne of the universe. The saga of the Kpelé translation was not over.

Fifty years later, in 1980, the doors to Guinea opened a crack and the first new missionary in 17 years entered the country. She was burdened for Bible translation but her ministry was restricted by government regulations to the Bible institute.

In 1981 the door cracked a bit wider and a new missionary couple arrived. Then, in 1984, the president of Guinea, Sekou Toure, died. The new government opened the door wide and invited missionaries into Guinea. God had answered our prayers.

Meanwhile, the Kpelé regional church president and a young pastor began translating the Bible. The young pastor went for further studies and his replacement didn't stick to it.

In 1986, I became involved in the project. But Satan specialized in frustration tactics at every turn. At the end of the school year I counted a discouraging total of eight actual hours of translation work.

In 1987, we were finally able to submit the Gospel of Matthew to the United Bible Society to publish as a booklet. The manuscript came back with 68 pages of punctuation questions and spelling corrections. (The manuscript had been typed manually with four carbons!)

While I was home on furlough, I procured a laptop computer complete with accessories. I also learned how the Wycliffe Bible translators devel-

oped computing to expedite the translation process.

I returned to Guinea. At last I was released to
transfer to the Kpelé forest. Teaching our translators computing was both fun and frustration. I,
who didn't know much myself, was trying to teach
others. We learned together.

Then the government revised the national alpha-
bet. That meant that I would have to revise our al-
phabet and prepare the new non-European
characters. While I was doing that, an electrical
brown-out "fried" the AC computer adaptor. It was
five months before we received the replacement.

After finally getting the new characters inserted,
there was a glitch in the font software. Another
nine months of international correspondence to
correct the problem. Meanwhile, the translation
continued.

And then, at last, showers of blessing. We received new software and a new computer. With
the use of a second borrowed computer, we now
had three going every day to catch up on the
backlog of keyboarding.

In August 1991, with great rejoicing, we submitted the New Testament manuscript to the United
Bible Society. (We still had not received our Gospel of Matthew booklet.) Seven months later, we
received a letter asking when we intended to submit the manuscript.

We were numb with shock.

So we submitted a second copy, again hand-de-
livered by a missionary to the United Bible Society center.

Again, another seven months later, we received
another letter: "Why didn't you respond to the

letter of February 1992? Where is the New Testament manuscript?"

Shock—and anger.

This time I submitted a "please sign and return" form with the two manuscript diskettes. The missionary courier returned in a week with the signed, dated and stamped receipt form and a letter: "The files of Matthew, Mark, Luke and John are electronically corrupted. Please re-submit these files ASAP."

We submitted them and received another signed, dated and stamped receipt form.

And we waited.

In June 1994 we were notified that the Gospel of Matthew booklet in Kpelé had been shipped from the printer in Hong Kong to Guinea.

We waited.

I am writing this in January 1995. No one knows where in the world our Gospel of Matthew booklet is—Equatorial Guinea? Guinea-Bissau? Ghana, Africa? Papua New Guinea in the South Pacific? or Guyana in South America? Or, who knows, maybe even in a corner of the central post office in Conakry, Republic of Guinea?

And the New Testament? It is mired in a confusing stream of corrections and recorrections and faxes and more faxes. It is evident that Satan doesn't want God's Word in the hands of the Kpelé people.

And from all I've heard, our trials as a translation team are common. Please pray for Bible translators around the world.

> *"[S]o is my word that goes out from my mouth:*
> *It will not return to me empty,*
> *but will accomplish what I desire*
> *and achieve the purpose for which I sent it."*
> Isaiah 55:11

# BREAKDOWN IN SALDOU

## GUINEA, WEST AFRICA————————————

### P. Alan Clason

As a teacher at the Telekoro Bible Institute in Guinea, West Africa, I try to model biblical truths as well as talk about them. This commitment led to a very interesting student/professor weekend evangelism trip to Saldou, a village about 30 miles from the institute.

We left Friday afternoon after classes. The 30-mile trip took three hours because of the conditions of the roads. Many of the interior roads in Guinea are nothing more than hand-carved paths. The road to Saldou was no exception—very rocky and filled with ruts.

However, we arrived without incident, met the pastor and traveled with him to another village where he had prearranged an outdoor evangelistic meeting.

The whole village turned out to hear the preaching and see the gospel film. When the pastor gave the invitation to receive Christ, three people responded. We arrived back at Saldou late that night tired but rejoicing in God's grace for the three new believers.

Saturday evening, the same scenario was played out. This time, four villagers responded to the call to receive Christ.

Sunday morning we participated in the morning worship service at Saldou. All seven of the new believers were there. They had left their villages early Sunday morning to walk to the meeting.

After the morning service and noon meal, it was time to return to the Bible institute. We packed the car and left about 2 p.m., hoping to arrive home by dark.

About five miles down the road we stopped at a village to greet the local pastor and church members. As I stepped out of the car, one of the villagers pointed under the car. Diesel fuel was pouring out of the gas tank. Apparently we had driven over one too many rocks.

Never being very knowledgeable about mechanical things, my first inclination was to jump back in the car and race the 25 miles home, hoping to beat the flow of fuel. But while I was contemplating this plan of action, one of the Guineans, who hated to see anything go to waste, put a large pan under the leak. The pan was full in about two minutes. Obviously the tank would have been empty long before we reached home.

The pastor invited us into his house and offered to help in any way he could. I told him I really needed to try to get home because my wife would be worried. He told me he had a moped that he would loan me but I should know that the brakes didn't work very well and it really didn't have enough power to climb hills. He suggested that when I got to a steep hill I should get off and walk the moped to the top, all the while trying to rev the throttle so the motor wouldn't die. I left the village with visions of my wife's surprise when I came rolling into Telekoro on a beat-up moped.

Sure enough, the moped couldn't climb the first hill. I jumped off and ran alongside it up the hill. At the top I jumped back on and headed down the hill, forgetting for the moment that the brakes didn't work. I almost killed myself when I hit a rock full speed.

About a mile further along, the moped died. I pedaled and pedaled to try to get it started, but to no avail. Something wasn't working, and with my lack of mechanical ability I had no idea what the problem might be. I pushed the vehicle to the next village and asked a man to keep it in his hut until I could return.

During the next three hours I walked about eight miles. I saw no one on the road except a few pedestrians like myself. Finally I reached another village with a Mission church.

"Does anyone here have a motorcycle I can borrow?" I asked.

The only person in the area that had a bike was not home. But someone said he had heard a motorcycle coming down the road and had stopped and asked the driver if he would give me a ride home. I hurried back out to the road grateful that the end of this nightmare was now in sight.

The man and his girlfriend were waiting for me on a small dirt bike.

"Get on!" they said, looking at me rather quizically.

I climbed onto the luggage rack behind the African lady and we traveled triple for the next 15 miles. We soon arrived at another church. They dropped me off at the front door and I borrowed the pastor's motorcycle to get back to the Bible institute by nightfall.

I have always felt somewhat inadequate in situations beyond my control. That day God reminded me that, after all, He is the One who is in control. Even in Saldou. Even for the future.

*"Have I not commanded you? Be strong
and courageous. Do not be terrified;
do not be discouraged, for the LORD your God will be
with you wherever you go."*
Joshua 1:9

# ROMANCE, MISSIONARY STYLE

## Anonymous

One night, 10 years ago, I achieved my personal best. Yes, I made history as I personally, single-handedly rewrote the definition of romance.

Up until that night, if I had thought of it at all, I suppose I would have defined romance by using one cliché after another—you know, the blazing fire, the bearskin rug, the spouse of my dreams. But that night I came up with a definition of romance which satisfied me completely then and which still, 10 years later, makes my heart do a fancy number—16th notes, all stacatto.

That important night found me far from my home and native land. I was living in Africa, along with my wife and baby daughter. At that particular time, my work had taken me away from major centers, at least five hours away from any electricity, into a rural area where many of the younger village children were seeing a white man for the first time in their lives.

For eight days I had seen only African faces. I had spoken nothing but an African language. My diet had been manioc root, rice and various forms of bananas. My drinks had been boiled water tasting strongly of an open fire and a fair amount of absolutely unbelievably awful coffee. My bed had been a sleeping bag laid on a shelf of bamboo.

The eight days had come to an end and as I nudged the jeep homeward my mind was peaceful, my heart content. The trip had been a success and I was filled with love and gratitude to my African hosts. But as one dusty kilometer followed another and as the equatorial darkness gently closed in around me, my thoughts were more and more focused on the journey's end.

I knew what was waiting for me—the pretty brick house with its cool stone floor, fresh bread straight out of the oven, the smell of perfect coffee, the bathtub waiting to be filled with hot water and the smooth sheets covering a firm mattress. I knew I'd get to tiptoe into my baby's room, watch her sleep and feel like the richest man in the world.

And even though all of that would bring me as close to heaven as any earthbound mortal could hope to be, I knew there was something waiting which was an even more exquisite pleasure. I'd get to sit across from my soulmate, my closest friend, my companion and we could start to share as only lovers can.

We'd use our beautiful mother tongue, the language I'd missed so much during the past eight days. And I'd tell her all about my trip and she'd tell me all about what had gone on in my absence. We'd laugh, we'd joke, we might even cry. And sometime in the midst of all that talk, surrounded by familiar space, I'd know that I was tasting romance at its absolute finest.

Yes, I redefined romance that night as I drove along a dark African road. From that time forward it would mean the sharing of hearts and minds in a loved, familiar place.

> *"Find a wife and you find a good thing;*
> *it shows that the LORD is good to you."*
> Proverbs 18:22 (Good News Bible)

# CANNIBAL VALLEY

## IRIAN JAYA, INDONESIA

### Mary Catto

**B**iak is a small coral island off the coast of Irian Jaya (formerly known as New Guinea), the second largest island in the world. It was here General McArthur based his air combat forces during World War II.

Desolate, bleak, hot, damp—all of these words described Biak in those post-war days. The ruins of 750 warplanes lay in mammoth dumps. One large shack by the sea boasted cooking and dining facilities for the Americans. There was a hospital with beds draped with mosquito nets. And there were swarms of mosquitoes to go along with the nets.

Meals consisted of rice, fishheads and greens from the local *pasangrahan* (hotel). Somewhat unfriendly bugs and lizards and curious but friendly nationals watched our every move.

Biak was my initial landing spot in the fascinating country of Indonesia. I was told that it would be my home until an amphibian plane could be chartered from the Dutch Navy to take my companions and me into the interior.

Each day began with a ride in a rusty, left-over weapons' carrier. Our destination? The warehouse

41

by the sea. Warehouse? Could it really be called that? Surrounded by open fencing and covered by a roof of discarded rusty zinc, also left over from the war, this dilapidated structure was where we spent hour upon hour in unbearable heat unpacking our drums, trunks and crates. The unpacked outfit was then repacked into gunny sacks for the anticipated airlift to our new home in the interior.

The relics of past foreign influence were everywhere. A certain little boy walked by every day with his catch of fish. One day he ventured close to where I was typing and began to sing "Pistol Packin' Mama" and "Hello Jo, Come on Baby, Let's Go"—all of which he had learned from American GIs. I couldn't help but smile at the incongruity of the situation.

Then there was the Chinese all-purpose store where we could buy rice, dried fish, cloth, matches, salt, canned meat, kerosene and margarine in five-pound tins. Smells of salt water and the coral reef permeated the air, making everything in our little house—and the makeshift hospital—both damp and musty.

It was at that hospital where the generator sputtered as I was having a much-dreaded and unexpected appendectomy. The four-hour operation by kerosene lamp light left me with a four-inch scar—one inch for every hour.

Everyone, including my partner Marion Doble and I, wanted to get out of Biak as quickly as possible. But God kept us there for six long weeks. Finally, a Catalina flying boat was made available to fly us into the interior. I was permitted to go along only for the ride this time because of my health and the fact that there was as yet no radio communication with the outside world where we were going.

Enaratoli! Wissel Lakes! Lake Paniai! No imagination, however wild or romantic, could describe what we would meet on that eventful, long-awaited day.

The familiar phrase, "buckle up," had not been invented when Marion and I climbed into the glass blister of the military flying boat which would take us to this exotic place. The blister once housed guns, but this day it accommodated gunny sacks, suitcases and small crates—all full of our belongings—upon which we perched precariously as we viewed the exquisite jungle scenery below.

Azure skies, beautiful serpentine rivers winding through dense jungle—they were only a preview of the alpine Lake Paniai, our anticipated landing spot.

Excited and scared to death hardly described our feelings as we touched down for the first time on the watery site and were helped into a hollowed-out log occupied by three scantily clothed women and one barely clothed man, all standing up in the boat.

There hardly seemed to be room for Marion and me. But, squeezing sideways into the wet and muddy dugout, I began to wonder if I would ever get out. And what would happen to me if we capsized before then?

The handmade oars began to fly as the women, one sitting on the back of the boat steering and two rigorously paddling from the sides, geared up. Directly in front of me stood the man, issuing orders.

Enaratoli at last! People, people, people, coming down the mountain in droves—unclothed, unbathed, unlovely, with an unknown and unwritten language. What could we do? How could we do it? How could we give them the most precious treasure they would ever own?

And the language. Could I learn it? How would I learn it?

My thoughts were suddenly interrupted by a most unusual welcome committee.

"*Jagamo* (woman)! *Nogei* (friend)!" Muddy hands reaching from all directions to touch our white skin.

I looked into the smiling faces and big brown eyes and heard "*nogei, nogei*" over and over again. I was their friend. They were my friends. I felt strangely welcome in this unusual land.

The pilot said we would spend only one hour at Enarotali. I wanted to see the Mission village where I would eventually live. Mud oozed from my shoes and splashed on my clothes as I made my way up the slippery trail surrounded by my "friends."

I tried to see the houses, but the people were swarming around in such crowds it was almost impossible. Muddy hands continued to reach for my clothes, my arms, my hair. The chatter was ear-piercing. Everyone was talking at once.

Suddenly, as we stood on the small porch of one of the houses, an elderly, gray-haired man made his way through the crowd to where Marion and I stood. He reached his hand into the greasy net bag he was carrying and pulled out a freshly roasted sweet potato.

Dusting it off, he broke it in half and gave a piece to each of us.

*No, I can't do this,* I thought as I slowly extended my hand. *Surely it is covered with germs coming from that greasy bag and those unwashed hands.*

But something inside of me said, "Take a bite." I did. It was delicious. Everyone screamed with delight and began again to chant "Nogei, nogei, nogei." So many things to see. So many things to smell. *How can I live with this kind of people?* I wondered almost aloud.

Then it was as if the Lord spoke to me with four little words, "For whom Christ died. For whom Christ died." These, too, were precious in His sight. Jesus died for them, too.

My eyes brimmed with tears. How long they had waited to hear the wonderful story of Jesus and His love for them! From that moment, God planted in my heart a supernatural love that has never left.

How sad I was to climb back into the blister and return to Biak for the appendectomy. When would I return to my friends? Only God knew.

One year and nine days later, I landed again on Lake Paniai, this time to stay. The welcome was different. The plane anchored out in the water and we were greeted by the local government official who took us ashore in his rubber dinghy. Hundreds of people were waiting to give us a most royal welcome.

As we neared the shore, I could hear the young men from the newly opened Bible school singing, "Pass me not, O gentle Savior, Hear my humble cry. While on others Thou art calling, do not pass me by."

How long, how very long these people had been passed by. But now, they, too, would have the opportunity to hear the good news of salvation. They, too, would experience God's power to redeem them by the precious blood of His Son.

Now, nearly 50 years later, throughout Irian Jaya, in more than 2,000 Christian and Missionary Alliance churches, 300,000 people meet to worship the living God.

> *"For God so loved the world that he gave*
> *his one and only Son, that whoever believes*
> *in him shall not perish but have eternal life."*
> John 3:16

# CARJACKED AT GUNPOINT

**CONGO, AFRICA**

## Carolyn Erbst

The day had begun in a fairly ordinary way. I was enjoying my new apartment in a safer part of the city of Brazzaville, Congo, where widespread violence due to civil unrest had forced me to relocate.

I had just called my fellow missionary, Tammy Noel, on the two-way radio to arrange to go with her to a women's meeting that afternoon at the Mfilou church. Even though the church was located in a neighborhood devastated by looting, the church itself had remained intact. Since the city had been calm for a while, we felt we could once again venture into that area to encourage the Christians who had suffered so much.

One of the verses Tammy had been highlighting in our Bible studies was from Proverbs: "Trust in the LORD with all your heart and lean not on your own understanding; in all your ways acknowledge him, and he will make your paths straight" (3:5-6). She had also been teaching the women a little chorus, the English translation as follows: "I have confidence in my Lord along the road / I have confidence in my Lord and He holds my hand / Going through the storm, my heart is at peace / I have

47

confidence in my Lord and I am protected." Little did we know that we were going to need to experience that peace and protection firsthand on this day.

I was enjoying using an air-conditioned car that belonged to another missionary family, but I knew this would be one of my last trips in it since they were due back from furlough in just two weeks. I drove over to the Noels to pick up Tammy and three-and-a-half-year-old Katie. Off we went to Mfilou.

As we approached the church's neighborhood, we were confronted by a barricade. We stopped. The guards were happy, they said, that we were going to church to pray and asked if we would pray for them as well.

Farther down the road we noticed a group of men standing by a boarded-up store. As we approached, a soldier came out of a small shack and fired his automatic rifle into the air. We stopped.

Before we could finish identifying ourselves, 25 to 30 men surrounded our car, pushing and shouting, their faces staring menacingly through the windows. We tried to make it clear that we were American missionaries going to a church meeting. (There was a lot of animosity toward French nationals at that time, so we wanted to emphasize our North American roots.)

In the midst of the melee, one of the soldiers said, "Don't worry, I am just going to shoot down by your tires." With that, he fired twice, evidently trying to take control of the situation and restore order. But it was already too late.

The mob was shouting for us to get out of the car. We did. In the midst of all the noise and confusion and different languages, it was hard to figure out just why they were detaining us and what they wanted. One man tried to get my address, assuring me that he would get the car back to us. It was then I realized they wanted the car!

I reached into my purse to get my address. The men started trying to snatch anything they could. One hand grabbed a couple of bills. One was handed back to me. It was comforting to know there were some in the crowd who were taking our side in this surprising—and dangerous—turn of events.

Another man came up and offered to take us home. He tried to lead Tammy away from the car. She shouted, "No, my daughter is in there." Some of the crowd was reaching in, trying to loosen Katie's carseat. I looked on in disbelief as this normally sensitive child remained calm in all the confusion. Apparently God's angels were surrounding us, blocking out the noise and tension from her eyes and ears.

Another hand tried to yank the gold chain off Tammy's neck. She finally took it off and gave it to the man in hopes it would buy enough time to get Katie out of the car. Someone else demanded her watch and wedding ring. Another man stepped in and reprimanded the thief, telling him not to do that.

A soldier finally grabbed Tammy by the arm and led her to the top of the knoll. Within minutes, Katie was placed in her mother's arms.

In the meantime, I was reaching into the car for the basket carrying my Bible, hymnbook and two-way radio. But other hands were still reaching with mine. In the confusion, my glasses were

knocked off. I screamed as I grabbed for them.
This caused the men to back off. I quickly grabbed
the basket. Another sympathetic man reached in
and pulled out the tire jack before leading me to
his car.

From our vantage point in the rescuer's car we
watched as about 20 people crowded into and
onto the hood and roof of our car and drove off.
We expected never to see the vehicle again. I felt
sick at the thought of the returning missionaries
arriving to discover they had lost their vehicle.

A mob was still milling around Tammy's door,
yelling at her and giving her messages to give to
President Clinton. Eventually, as the neighborhood disappeared behind us, Tammy and I began
to praise the Lord. Although the car had been
taken, we were unharmed and safely on our way
home.

Our rescuer was livid over the whole incident
and insisted on reporting it immediately to the
authorities. We told him that being missionaries
and foreigners we really didn't want to do anything until we had spoken to Tammy's husband,
the field director, and also to the American embassy. But we were a captive audience, so we
waited in the car while the driver went to the police to plead our case.

Two days later, the vehicle was returned with
only minor damage. We were told that rebel soldiers felt they were being ignored by the authorities so were choosing to be disruptive to make
their presence felt. Stealing the vehicle had suited
their attention-getting agenda.

And little Katie? She never talked about the incident. Tammy believes the Lord wiped that awful

memory from her mind. Perhaps in eternity we will see just how many angels were surrounding our car in Mfilou that day.

> *"Trust in the LORD with all your heart*
> *and lean not on your own understanding;*
> *in all your ways acknowledge him,*
> *and he will make your paths straight."*
> Proverbs 3:5-6

# PRISONERS OF THE LORD

## Herbert and Ruth Clingen

It was February 23, 1945. We, along with our young son, Bobby, were among the 2,147 people liberated by the 11th Airborne of the U.S. Army from the Los Banos internment camp in the Philippines. The day of our liberation was to have been our last day on earth. Our captors were planning to exterminate all the prisoners of war in their camp.

Three years earlier we had been forced to the Islands from our mission field in Laos because of the impending conflict with the Japanese. For one whole year we hid from them in the jungles of Mindanao Island. Then our missionary staff of 33, including children, were suddenly captured. We moved from one camp to another over the next 25 months, surviving on reduced rations, no news from home and in close confinement.

Our first camp was in Davao where we joined several hundred others who had been there since the outbreak of the hostilities. Our home was a bedbug-infested former cabaret building. The food was poor and inadequate.

Suddenly, without advance notice, our captors decided to transport us aboard a troop ship to an undisclosed destination. Several days later, having buried one of our men at sea, we arrived in Manila and joined several thousand other internees. Conditions here were better, partly due to the distribution of Red Cross comfort kits including food supplies, soap and other necessities.

We were housed in the abandoned but now crowded classrooms of Santo Tomas University. Disease was rampant. Herb came down with severe attacks of malaria. Bobby had trench mouth, measles, whooping cough and colitis. Herb and I both contracted painful dengue fever.

At the end of four months we learned of a new camp located 45 kilometers south of Manila. We applied for a transfer and joined several hundred others there. It was located on the agricultural campus at Los Banos where the Japanese had constructed 20 barracks, each accommodating 100 prisoners.

By this time, our American forces were gaining air supremacy. The enemy took revenge by cutting our already meager food supply to two meals a day. With weight loss and limited strength, we could perform only the most necessary tasks.

Then, with an air of mystery, all the guards left the camp. Six days later, with no explanation, they returned. In the interim, however, our men had discovered large quantities of rice and molasses that had been kept from us. It soon became clear that for almost a year a deranged Japanese officer had denied us food, unnecessarily restricting the daily ration to 550 calories per person.

One morning, in desperation, the missionaries gathered for prayer, pleading with God to intervene in our desperate situation. The answer came 24 hours later.

The next morning, just before the daily roll-call bell sounded, we heard the roar of planes overhead. Within moments, paratroopers jumped directly overhead while Filipino troops, who had surrounded the camp during the night, annihilated the guards.

Amphibious tanks crossed the lake and roared onto the campus. In the confusion and jubilation that followed, Herb, Bobby and I boarded a tank and slowly passed over the barbed wire to freedom. Trucks and ambulances were waiting to take us on the final leg of our journey to an abandoned Filipino prison now occupied by American forces.

There, the weakest and pregnant women like myself received special care. One week later I gave birth to a beautiful, healthy baby girl.

In 1995 we celebrated our 50th wedding anniversary. After these many years, the Psalmist's thoughts are our thoughts, too.

*"For thou, O God, hast proved us: thou hast tried us, as silver is tried. Thou broughtest us into the net; thou laidst affliction upon our loins.*
*Thou hast caused men to ride over our heads; we went through fire and through water: but thou broughtest us out into a wealthy place. . . .*
*I will pay thee my vows, Which my lips have uttered, and my mouth hath spoken, when I was in trouble. . . .*
*Blessed be God, which hath not turned away my prayer, nor his mercy from me."*
Psalm 66:10-14, 20 (KJV)

# CHANTA'S PRAYER

### N. David Ens

It was winter and in France winter means rain—cold rain that sometimes turns to sleet.

Chanta, a Cambodian refugee and single parent, was making her way back to the Camembert apartments where she lived with her three sons. The structure is so called because it resembles two wheels of camembert cheese on their sides.

The complex is located in the Paris suburb of Noisy le Grand, close to a major shopping mall. It was from that mall that Chanta was returning that evening, her hands full of groceries, her umbrella jostled by the wind.

From the corner of her eye she caught a glimpse of a dark-complexioned youth in the shadow of an archway. She passed by, thinking he was simply seeking shelter from the drizzle. Then, the sound of footsteps and Chanta felt her purse being wrenched from her grasp.

"*Au secours!* (Help!)" she screamed as the boy ran off.

Two would-be Samaritans took chase. But they soon returned with nothing to offer but their condolences. Tearfully Chanta made her way back to her flat. Gone were the documents which gave her the legal right to be in France. Gone were her credit cards, her money, her checkbook, her expensive new prescription glasses and her house keys.

Fortunately she had left the boys at home and would be able to gain entry. This was little comfort, however, knowing that she had no way to have another key made and a replacement lock would cost nearly $300.

As Chanta rode the elevator to the sixth floor, she called out to the only One she knew could really help her—Jesus. Only He could set things right. After putting the groceries away and the children to bed, she retired for the night.

The next day, Chanta made her way to the police station to report the theft. While she gave her report, the desk sergeant was interrupted to book two young men arrested for possession of stolen goods. Among the incriminating evidence in their possession were two of Chanta's credit cards.

"Thank you, God," she prayed quietly as the officer handed her the cards.

Back at home, Chanta was informed that the train station had called. They were holding her purse and her keys. Again, she thanked God.

One more call came that day from the caretaker of a nearby apartment complex. He explained that, while cleaning the grounds, he had found her identification papers and two checkbooks. Chanta raced to reclaim these precious items, her heart giddy with joy. Truly her Savior had come through for her again.

That evening she took inventory of what had been lost and what had been found. The cash was gone and so were her precious glasses. She would need to reorder them and perhaps even be required to have her eyes tested again.

The following day, at the optometrist's office, Chanta was pleased to find that her test results were in the computer and she had only to order new glasses. She cringed as she paid for them, but it had to be done. Now she only needed to wait the week or so while they were made.

During that week Chanta had the opportunity to tell her story at the Cambodian Evangelical Church in Marne la Vallee. The congregation joined their prayers with hers.

One week had gone by since the robbery. Chanta was at home when the phone rang. A Frenchman identified himself and asked if she was Madame Noun Chanta. When she confirmed this, he went on to say that a pair of glasses had been turned into the lost and found at the mall and that from the receipt inside the case, they had traced them through the optometrist back to her.

Chanta ran to the office to make her claim. Another brief prayer of praise. With her glasses back in her possession she realized there was now no need to order—and pay for—the new pair. When the clerk agreed to refund her money, Chanta breathed yet another "thank you" to the Lord.

The following Sunday when Pastor Va Po asked if anyone had a word of praise, Chanta recounted her story. And as Chanta sat down, the congregation applauded, not for Chanta, but for the great God who had answered Chanta's prayer.

> *"Ask and you will receive,*
> *and your joy will be complete."*
> John 16:24

# A LITTLE PAIN— A LOT OF GAIN

## CONGO, AFRICA

### Myra Brown

*Ah, Sunday morning! Sleep a while. Carry on a deep conversation with Smokey, my cat, while settling into the recliner for my quiet time. Linger over that second cup of coffee. Enjoy putting on a pretty dress and giving a bit more time to my hair.*

Such is Sunday morning in the dreams of veteran missionary Carolyn Erbst. But what is the Sunday morning reality for this tall, gracious woman in Brazzaville, Congo?

Up at 6. A quick review of the lesson studied during the previous week. Devotions, breakfast, coolest dress she can find. Out the door by 7. Start up the cranky old Subaru and hope this will be one of its better days. Try to ignore the remnants of odor thanks to the untimely demise of three mice in the car's bowels.

Drive 20 minutes while carefully dodging the innumerable potholes filled with water hiding just how deep those holes really are. Park the car just south of a garbage pile, walk another block, arrive at the "church," a shelter made of roofing tin.

All of this is the prelude to Carolyn Erbst's demanding but rewarding day of ministry on an ordinary Sunday.

Her first class begins at 7:30 a.m., a class of four young men wanting to study the Bible in a serious way. They have enrolled in an extension study program and are working on a course about the abundant life.

From the beginning, this group has been a source of great blessing to Carolyn. The young men are hungry to know more of God's Word and it was they who chose the 7:30 start-up time on Sunday. They've asked that the one-hour class be extended to one-and-a-half hours so their questions can be handled in more detail.

Beyond questions related to the course, they bring practical concerns—how can I have a better devotional time with the Lord when I sleep in the living room of my brother's house and other family members are also up very early? What should I say to the Muslim man who works with me? These questions and many more come up often, making Carolyn feel very inadequate for her job.

Yet many times she has sensed God taking over the class and she can testify with Paul in Ephesians 3:20: "To him who is able to do immeasurably more than all we ask or imagine, according to his power that is at work within us."

With the class over by 9:30, Carolyn is already late for the service she attends in a nearby section of Brazzaville. She particularly enjoys the time of worship since it is her privilege to serve on the worship team there and she helps train the group.

Chugging home from church, Carolyn keeps her eye peeled for a gas station actually serving gas! Fuel shortages make keeping the tank full quite a challenge. A quick lunch, a short rest and Carolyn is once again backing her car onto the street to head for yet another section of the city.

Four women are waiting for her as she arrives. This discipleship class is studying foundational Bible truths. It is in French and requires a lot of personal study for Carolyn. Classes meet once a week for two hours.

One of Carolyn's four students is a 31-year-old woman named Suzanne. Married, with two children, Suzanne is also a full-time student studying psychology at the university. Even though her father led her to the Lord at the age of 11, she feels she had few chances to really grow in her faith since Congo's former Marxist regime permitted limited opportunities for children. So when Carolyn began teaching extension Bible courses at her church, Suzanne was quick to enroll.

Now, a year later, Suzanne continues to study the Bible at every opportunity despite her family responsibilities and her studies. One week, when all the church leaders were away and there was no one to preach on Sunday, Suzanne was asked to preach. People were blessed as they heard God's Word.

To Suzanne's great joy, God has also been working in the life of her husband Daniel. He has given himself to God. They pray together and they memorize the Scriptures required for their discipleship classes.

But their faith is being tested these days. Daniel, a government employee, hasn't received a salary for 15 months (except for December) and the family needs to give up the house where they have been living rent-free.

Both Suzanne and Daniel want to rent another house in the neighborhood so they can continue to host their respective discipleship classes. But paying rent is impossible without a salary. Carolyn is praying with Suzanne as she trusts God to work out this problem.

By 6 o'clock the class is coming to an end and the sun is starting to set on Brazzaville. Carolyn finishes the lesson on how to live in victory over sin and puts the key in her car door. She hopes this key won't break off in the lock like the last one did.

Darkness comes quickly on the equator and by the time a tired but happy Carolyn reaches home, it's already night. A full day of worship and Bible study. A demanding day, but such a rewarding one!

Knowing Monday will offer her some much-needed rest and relaxation, Carolyn settles down for a quiet evening with Smokey at her feet.

*"As long as it is day,*
*we must do the work of him who sent me.*
*Night is coming, when no one can work."*
John 9:4

# A DYAK STANDS UP FOR JESUS

BORNEO, INDONESIA

## Harry W. Post

The five-foot high veranda of the Dyak long-house was packed with brown bodies all seated on the floor. From below the rough-hewn planks eminated a cacophony of sounds: pigs, chickens, dogs and goats, all speaking in their native languages.

Since this meeting was in the evening, the familiar kerosene pressure lamp was called into action, droning on in the performance of its duty.

Beyond the reach of the lamp's glow, all was dark except for the odd flickering flame rising from inside a coconut shell full of pitch or containing an oil-soaked wick.

A full-moon canine choir pierced the eerie stillness of the jungle night. Soon human voices joined them in praise to the living God. The words were not mere words. These were spiritual truths that had been patiently and painstakingly implanted into darkened hearts.

Then, it was my turn. I had come here to preach and to teach, line upon line, precept upon precept. The crowd listened, seemingly undisturbed by the constant shifting around them.

As I concluded my message, I paused.

"Does anyone have a question or something to say?" I asked in my street-meeting voice so everyone could hear.

After what seemed like minutes, one of the group spoke. He began to launch a verbal attack on a young chief who was present. Calling him by name, the man accused the chief of dishonoring the tribe's reputation by becoming a Christian.

"You are not the leader you should be," he shouted at the young believer. "Your village is behind the times."

From my shadowy vantage point above the crowd, I watched the young chief's face, alert and tense in the glow of the lamp. Finally, the tirade came to an end. A strained silence engulfed the listeners. *What will happen now?* I wondered somewhat nervously.

Though relatively young and lacking the respect that would be due an elder, the subject of the attack was nevertheless a chief. I knew he had earned the gratitude of his tribal group for his skill as an arbitrator of peace. Some years before, there had been a head-hunting foray into his area by a distant tribe. A lingering longing for revenge had pervaded the village, but the young chief's patient intervention had deflected an explosive and distinctly un-Christian response.

The young man remained quiet for a few tension-filled moments. Then, slowly, deliberately, he rose to his feet. With consummate poise, he began to speak.

"I am glad to be mocked and ridiculed because of my faith in Jesus Christ," he said. "It is in Him I have found forgiveness for my sins, and from Him I have received peace of heart."

He took a deep breath, then continued.

"There was a time when I, too, worshiped the spirits and offered blood sacrifices. I, too, took part in ceremonies and rituals to ensure a good harvest and protection from evil spirits. But, through the power of Jesus Christ, I have been set free."

The chief's firm and courageous voice had reached to every corner of the longhouse veranda and beyond into the jungle night. There could be no doubt where he stood. His witness had been clear. He had taken his place in the heavenlies with Christ. He had fought a battle and won. He had proven he was God's man even in the midst of a human, but nevertheless satanic, attack. Although publicly mocked, he had given a memorable witness to the Christ living in him.

The pressure lamp droned on, its glow shrinking into the darkness. The people were silent.

Believers in many parts of the world endure both verbal and physical violence because of their faith in the Lord Jesus Christ. Spiritual combat is worldwide. Knowing this, we must give ourselves to intercessory prayer for all believers who suffer because they dare to stand up for Jesus.

> *"I am not ashamed of the gospel,*
> *because it is the power of God*
> *for the salvation of everyone who believes."*
> Romans 1:16

# DEAR MOM AND DAD

## ARGENTINA, SOUTH AMERICA————

### Mary Dellos

Hi! Hope everything's going well there in Helena. I can't believe it's been a year since we left the States! We can still remember those tearful good-byes. But God has been good to us.

In spite of the fact that we couldn't speak any Spanish before arriving in Costa Rica, now at least we can communicate a little. We graduated last night. Boy, was that a relief!

You won't believe how much the kids have grown. We are really excited about how well their Spanish is coming along. They probably speak better than we do!

Our neighbors, Coco and Marlen, have been such a blessing to us. They have had so much patience with our broken Spanish. Sometimes I don't understand why they befriended us. They just had a baby boy. He is darling. They have a lot of questions about Jesus. We share with them. Please pray for them. It will be hard to say good-bye.

Ashleigh and Ryan are really enjoying wrestling this year. Don't worry—they have a trained coach, a fellow missionary, who wanted to teach the kids how to wrestle. He considers it a ministry to them. They have had a lot of fun and done quite well.

Chelsea isn't into that kind of thing. She's still into pretty dresses. We bought her a native Costa Rican dress with the money you sent for her birthday. She loves it!

We had a great time with Don's parents. We went to the beach. It was beautiful and so relaxing! The kids loved being with them. Thanks for the Oreos! We gobbled 'em up!

Here we are again packing up for another major move. We've heard a lot about Argentina, but I'm not sure exactly what to expect. It's always different than what one thinks. At least we'll finally be on the mission field that God has called us to. It's kind of exciting and scary at the same time.

Thanks for your prayers. We love you and miss you a lot!


Hi! We arrived safely and there were several missionaries to greet us with the warm Argentine hug and kiss on the cheek. Even the men greet that way. We feel really blessed to be part of such a neat team of missionaries!

We stayed one month in Buenos Aires in a small apartment. It's a huge city—-about 13 million. I'm glad we'll be in a less populated place. Our field director and his wife took us to Santa Rosa, about an eight-hour drive from Buenos Aires. It's a really pretty city, surrounded by cattle farms. We hunted for a house to rent but there wasn't anything. Everything is for sale and the rents are outrageous. God is going to have to intervene. I know He will because He wants us in this city.

The church people welcomed us warmly with an *asado*—Argentine barbecue. It was delicious. At least we enjoy the food here. It's great! We are meeting in the home of one of the members. There are about 25 including the kids. They are all related. It could prove interesting! We were told that it will either be a blessing or a curse. Please pray with us in this situation.

We need to find a neutral place to meet. I think it will be difficult since the majority of the people here are against evangelicals.

I hate to go shopping because when we ask for something they always charge us at least 10 times more because they can hear our North American accent. I'm trying to remember, Dad, your advice about burning bridges, but I can't stand being taken advantage of. Pray for me!

We're excited about the kids' school. There are a few teachers who speak some English, so if the kids get confused maybe they'll get a little extra help. I'm a little concerned that Ashleigh is the only girl in her class. Ryan will do okay—his class is all boys. Chelsea is entering fourth grade with only the little bit of Spanish she learned in Costa Rica. Don and I definitely are not at the fourth grade level yet! It may be a hard adjustment for her. I just have to trust that God knows what's best for our kids. I'm enclosing a picture of their first day. They seem so small and innocent. I'm thankful God is with them!

Better close. I have lots to do. Our barrels still haven't arrived and we're still on foot. Walking everywhere is good exercise, but Santa Rosa is a city of 75,000 and the bus service is real sporadic. We do need a car.

I know I've given you lots of prayer requests. Can I give you one more? Pray for friends. It's pretty lonely here!

Sorry it's been a while since I wrote last. I guess I don't have any desire to do much of anything. I suppose it's normal to get depressed and feel lonely when you're so far away from everything familiar. I really look forward to receiving mail. Actually there have been days when I begged God to please make sure there's a letter in our mailbox.

One of the churches that adopted Ryan sent him a sweatshirt that says, "Chinook loves Ryan." I cried when I saw it. He doesn't even know those ladies and they cared enough about him to send that neat gift. He loves it! That really brightened my day!

I told you a few months ago about Raul and Silvia, the new couple in the church who have been so wonderful to us and just recently invited Jesus into their hearts. Well, they just moved last week to a city about 12 hours away. She was really the only one I felt like I could talk to and pray with. I had to question God: "Why Silvia? My only friend? What are you doing?" Seems like everything horrible happens at once. Sometimes I feel so stranded and isolated here.

Hopefully we'll get a car soon. I'm a nervous wreck taking the kids through the center of town on our bikes to get them to their gym class. It's getting cold. Don has been fighting bronchitis for a couple weeks. He broke his arm while he was playing soccer with the kids. He's a little discouraged, too!

Hi! It was great talking to you last night. It's a blessing having a phone! The car is running pretty good, but the Mission wants us to sell it before we come home for furlough.

Well, lots has changed since I last wrote. I can't believe the greatness of my God. He sure has taught me a lot these past five years and now we're coming home in a couple months.

We are so happy that we changed schools. Ashleigh has a wonderful school-friend named Andrea and she loves to go again. She also has a sweet friend at church named Daniela.

I think it's going to be really hard for Chelsea to leave her old school. She had adapted so well. They all tell us that she speaks beautiful Spanish. And guess what? She was at the top of her class and got to escort the flag at the end-of-year ceremony. That's a great honor in Argentina!

Ryan will miss Pablo a lot! They are together all the time! Even though Pablo is in a wheelchair, they play sports together. I never dreamed that Ryan would bond so closely with anyone. They really love each other.

The church is going well. We're finishing up the remodeling project. It's looking more like a church every day. The first church is growing now, too, since the family that caused so much division left. Actually both churches are working together to reach Santa Rosa for Christ. God has brought about healing and forgiveness. Satan has been defeated again! Praise God!

I have wonderful news. God has brought Raul and Silvia back. Don dedicated their baby girl last Sunday. Silvia is now one of my many friends. Isn't the Lord good?

God has not changed, but my perspective of Him has! The incredible way He brought about justice and unity in our situation is unbelievable! I believe so strongly that He has a plan for our lives and is faithful to bring us through the tough times and even bless our lives more than we could have hoped for. It's incredible!

You know, even though we really were the target of attack for several years, we were able to see fruit and the goodness of God. It'll be really hard to say goodbye again, this time to a group of people that at one time I wasn't sure that I'd actually be able to love. I praise God that my love for them goes deep. God has won another battle. Praise Him!

Thanks for always being there and for your love and support during the past five years. Can't wait to see you!

I love you,
Mary

> *" 'For I know the plans I have for you,'*
> *declares the LORD, 'plans to prosper you*
> *and not to harm you,*
> *plans to give you hope and a future.' "*
> Jeremiah 29:11

# GOD
# STOPS
# THE
# FIRE

**LAOS, SOUTHEAST ASIA**

## Donald H. Durling

It is the dry season early in the year 1966. I am walking in the company of a Christian of the Khamou tribe on a long trail in the northwestern part of Laos near the border with Thailand. We are still more than a day away from the end of our trip where I will again be home with my wife and children. We have to stay over one more night.

A little further along on this trail we will cross the ridge of another mountain where there is a Hmong village. That would be the logical place to spend the night except for the fact that the village is known for being sympathetic with the insurgent guerrillas. So we decide to go off the trail and stay in a village of the Mien tribe instead. We divert about an hour to the west and find ourselves at the village just before dusk.

As is common in the mountains, we are offered supper and a place to put our bedrolls for the night. Usually the chief of the village would be our host, but for some reason this night we are put into the house of the assistant chief. Later I find out that a renowned shaman from another area has come to cure the chief's wife of a sickness. It would certainly interrupt the process if the chief also hosted a missionary!

In the cycle of slash-and-burn agriculture as practiced in these mountains, the time has come to burn the fields. New areas of forest have been cut down and left to dry in preparation for being burned. Then, after the burning, when the rains start, rice will be planted in the newly cleared and burned land. In fact, as darkness falls, on the slope opposite us we can see a line of fire. It is less than a mile away but on the far side of a deep valley.

As usual, we eat the supper our host provides and, in place of just sitting and making small talk, we present the gospel. My fellow-traveler gives his testimony of how he was delivered from the bondage of witchcraft and spirit worship. Then I give a chronological presentation of the gospel from the preexistence of God, through the fall of Satan, creation, the fall of man, Christ's birth, His death on the cross for our sins and the resurrection.

The people of the Mien village listen politely but indicate nothing more than passing interest. The Mien are not an ignorant people. Many of their men have hired Chinese teachers and have learned to read the Chinese characters used in their witchcraft. That witchcraft has a powerful hold on them.

Before getting into my sleeping bag I go outside for a bit. The fire is still burning on the opposite slope, slowly edging down the mountain toward the dry valley gulch. It looks as though the fire is outside the perimeter of the field, burning the uncut forest. However, it isn't burning very fast because it is burning downhill. *No need to be concerned,* I tell myself.

Before I go back into the house to sleep, though, our host asks in a rather casual voice if my God can stop that fire. I swallow and tell him that yes, God can stop that fire. Now we are set up for a confrontation between the forces of darkness and the forces of light.

In the chief's house, just a short distance from where we are, a shaman is making contact with spirits to cure a sick person. Here, a few feet away, I am claiming that my God can stop a wildfire. I don't know if the assistant chief is asking the question on his own or if he is a spokesman and the whole village is watching to see what happens.

A lot is at stake here. If the fire stops, it will look good. But if perchance the fire crosses the dry gulch and starts racing up the mountain we are on, toward the village we are in, we might have to run for our lives in the middle of the night. I'm not sure I would be openly blamed for the loss of the village, but I might be. After all, I entered the village when a famous shaman was making contact with spirits and then made the statement that my God could stop the fire.

I pray earnestly that God will stop the fire. And I start looking for rainclouds in the moonlight. No rainclouds are in sight. And there isn't much likelihood that any will appear. This is, after all, the dry season.

As a matter of form, I unroll my sleeping bag and try to go to sleep. But the fire is so close that I can hear it crackling on the facing slope. I drop off into a fitful sleep.

Within minutes I awake to hear the fire still crackling. I silently pray again.

Throughout the first part of the night I wake up

about every 20 minutes, hear the crackling fire, look at my watch, pray and go back to sleep.

At 3:20 a.m. I wake up to hear the fire still crackling. I pray again and turn over for another fitful 20 minutes of sleep. At 3:40 I wake up and hear no more crackling. I go back to sleep until dawn.

After we are all up and getting ready to leave in the morning, our host tells us that the fire burned all the way down the mountain to the dry valley-bottom, but it didn't cross.

I thank the Lord and walk on toward home. The seed has been sown in another Mien village.

> *"Answer me, O LORD, answer me,*
> *so these people will know that you,*
> *O LORD, are God. . . ."*
> 1 Kings 18:37

# GOD'S MIRACLE

## GABON, West Africa

### Enid Miller

The sun was rapidly going down as it does in the tropics. The secondary school students, as well as many others, had already flowed in and out of our newly opened bookstore/reading room in Moanda, a lovely manganese mining center of Gabon in equatorial Africa.

Suddenly, rock-and-roll music blared out from the bar next door. I sighed. *What benefit will the bookstore offer in this atmosphere?* I wondered. *I might as well close up and go home.* At that moment, God brought very clearly to mind a word of advice offered by a Gabonese friend the night before. It was just one word: "Adjust!"

Night had already fallen when Madeleine had dropped in after work as a cashier in the mining company's general store. This was one of her frequent visits. We had been praising God together when the bar's raucous music bellowed forth. I groaned in exasperation. Madeleine dropped her head for a moment, then looked up sympathetically.

"Sister," she said quietly, "the bar is here to stay. Adjust!" And now, less than 24 hours later, her words were ringing in my ears.

As I reflected in the darkened store, I felt a powerful compulsion to lift my hands in praise and
worship to the Lord. I walked up and down the
aisles, my thoughts tuned heavenward. God's
presence seemed to fill the room. Then, to my
amazement, I heard His voice speaking deep
within my spirit: "Don't close. Someone is coming."

From a distance the sound of quiet voices became increasingly audible. I could see five men approaching, their eyes fixed on the bar, their faces
aglow with anticipation.

Then, just as they were about to pass the bookstore, one of them came to an abrupt halt. He
lifted his head and read in a clear and distinct
voice the sign above the entrance: Libraire Evan-
gelique (Evangelical Bookstore).

"I wonder what goes on in there," he said turning to the others questioningly. "Let's take a
look." Reluctantly his friends followed him inside.

I walked over to them.

"*Bon soir* (good evening)," I said with a smile.

"What do you do here?" one asked.

"Many things," I replied. "Could I invite you to
sit down?"

Evidencing some interest, they followed me to
the far end of the room where I had placed some
folding chairs and a blackboard for just such an
occasion.

For over two hours I shared God's love in sending His Son Jesus so that they could have eternal
life. The men bombarded me with questions
which I answered the best I could. Then it all
came to an abrupt halt. There was silence! I decided to seize the moment and invite them to re-

ceive Christ as their Lord and Savior. All five immediately responded, "Yes, that is what we want."

One of them, however, added quietly, "This path is the one I am going to follow, but there are things in my life that I must straighten out!" He had clearly understood God's message to his heart.

By then the hour was late. We formed a circle and worshiped God together, punctuating the time with another final moment of awesome silence.

As we headed toward the door, one of the men turned to me.

"This has been a miracle!" he said. "We are here on business from Libreville. Tonight is our last night in Moanda."

A miracle? Yes! God's miracle! He had used the raucous music from the bar next door to accomplish His miracle.

*"Go into all the world*
*and preach the good news to all creation."*
Mark 16:15

# A GIRL LIKE ESTHER

## MALI, West Africa————————————

### Doloris Burns Bandy

"**I** wonder where Benjamin is going so fast this early morning," remarked my husband Tom as the local pastor sped by at breakneck speed down the sandy path to another part of the village.

"Perhaps just to the bush for his morning ride," I laughingly retorted. The "bush" in these parts of the sub-Sahara meant thorn trees!

"No, he was going in the wrong direction for that," Tom replied, worry lines creasing his forehead.

"Oh, don't worry," I said. "You'll know soon enough if there is a problem."

These trips to the bush with a family of six for village-to-village literacy and Bible classes and evangelism among the Dogons required detailed preparation. It meant baking dozens of cookies, multiple loaves of banana bread, twice-toasted bread, as well as enough other goodies to last a week or more or until they dried out in the arid desert air.

To round out our diet we could count on scrawny, tough chickens and perhaps a rabbit or bush fowl that Tom and my son delighted to hunt. But there would be no fresh fruit or vegetables.

Added to these food staples were clothes, games and toys as well as books and other school supplies. Water bags, kerosene lanterns and folding chairs adorned the outside of the truck. And, of course, the family pets squeezed in between someone and something.

While Tom taught the first classes and the kids went on a search for a donkey to ride, I began the tailgate dispensary. Word travels fast in the desert. The lines grew longer and more demanding each day. Yet these simple acts of kindness often opened hearts to receive the message of the Great Physician.

Literacy classes with the women got underway after the morning food came out for the men and their families. I carried my folding chair to the well-ventilated cornstalk shelter with wall to wall sand flooring. And I waited!

The women arrived at their leisure, one at a time, babies on their backs and usually at least one toddler by their feet. I was always amazed that in spite of numerous distractions these women actually did learn to read.

Lunch time arrived.

"Well, what did you find out?" I asked as Tom and I sat down at the table.

"You won't believe this," he answered. "Remember the teenaged girl in your class, Yalei? Well, her dad, a strong fetishist threatened to beat her to death if she attended classes again. Benjamin didn't see her at the sun-up prayer time. He was so scared that he went to check it out."

"What happened? Had the father killed her? What did Benjamin find?"

"Hold it," Tom said. "One question at a time. No, he did not kill her, but she was beaten, locked in the house and threatened."

Several weeks later, back home from our trip, I heard the familiar clap of hands at the front door.

"Madame, *dige nai po,*" a voice called. I replied, "*O wou, mainiye gini do* (hello and welcome)."

I recognized the short, middle-aged church elder from the village where we had recently held classes. The young girl with him was Yalei. I invited them in.

The lengthy Malian greetings finally over, the elder proceeded to tell me that he had clandestinely brought Yalei to attend girls' school. Like the underground system during the Civil War, Christians along the way had hidden the two of them by day and they had traveled by night.

Yalei joined the nearly 100 girls already packed into inadequate dorms, sleeping several on a small grass mat. But she didn't seem to care. For the first time she was free—and happy. For Yalei this was paradise to be able to sing, to play, to study and to pray with other young Christian girls.

But the dream was soon shattered!

Within days I heard another knock at the door. This time, a gruff and unfamiliar voice bellowed the greetings. This time I did not recognize the obviously agitated stranger. Tom joined me and we invited the man into the house.

"I want my daughter back," he demanded. "You Christians kidnapped my daughter."

To comply with culture, we quickly sent for the pastor and other elders to join us and hear the "words" of Yalei's father. Yalei came, too, and sat quietly listening to the terrifying outburst.

"If the Christians do not give back my daughter I will return to Dangutenu, tear down the church, burn the Christians' houses, beat the pastor and any others I can find," he threatened.

Yalei had a decision to make. The Christians back in her village were now her people. If she opted to stay and enjoy the Christian love and freedom that she now had, her friends would suffer. If she returned, however, she would be tortured by her cruel father.

Yalei chose to return in order to save the Christians.

It would be a three-day trek descending the narrow rocky cliff trail and transversing deep sandy paths to reach her village. Like the biblical Esther before her, Yalei had made one request to the pastor: "Please ask the Christians here and those you meet to fast and pray for me."

Yes, Yalei was beaten nearly to death and kept a prisoner for weeks. But gradually she resumed the routine of village life—drawing water, cooking, going to market—but never to church.

It was a special market day in a nearby village. Yalei made the trip to buy supplies for the family. But instead of returning home, she continued on to another town. There the Christians once again gave her shelter.

She arrived several days later at our station, tired and exhausted. This time, the father could not blame the Christians. Yalei had returned alone. And this time, she stayed. She completed the school courses. When she was baptized with many of the other girls, she fittingly asked to now be called Esther.

Esther once again broke with custom and rejected the prearranged marriage made by her father. Instead, she married a handsome Bible school student. Since their graduation, Esther and her husband, Daniel, continue to serve the Dogon people.

> *"God is our refuge and strength,*
> *an ever-present help in trouble."*
> Psalm 46:1

# MAMA CHRISTINE

## GABON, West Africa

### Robert F. Greene, MD

**E**ven though her vision had been dimmed by cataracts, Mama Christine's memory was unclouded. One of the earliest converts in Gabon, she still remembered the days when her husband worked for Rev. Don Fairley, a pioneer missionary long since gone to his reward.

Now, as a widow from a poor village, Mama Christine never would have been able to afford eye surgery in the capital city of Libreville. But, in the preceding two years, Christoffel Blindenmission had helped The Christian and Missionary Alliance Hospital at Bongolo to develop an eye program, providing training and equipment.

In addition, Medical Ambassadors International began assisting a primary health care program to improve health and hygiene out in the villages. Terry Hotalen, one of our missionary nurses, made weekly visits to a nearby village and she had ferried patients to Bongolo, 24 miles away, for evaluation and care. Thanks to Terry's kindness, Mama Christine was one of those patients.

As an orthopedic surgeon, normally I would never do eye surgery. Filling in for Dr. David Thompson at Bongolo this year, however, I found that eye surgery was now part of the program. I had been taught to do cataract extractions 15 years earlier, but I was more than a little rusty. Mama Christine would be my third attempt at a cataract this year.

The first two had not gone well. Only one gained partial restoration of vision. Because it was six weeks since the last one, neither my confidence nor my proficiency were improving.

I had gathered more information about technique and medications and typed up a protocol to enhance the preparation for surgery. Still, I kept thinking of the statement of a veteran ophthalmologist in Africa: There is no place for the "occasional cataract surgeon." It is a delicate operation that requires frequent repetition to maintain the necessary skill. Was I doing the right thing for Mama Christine?

Slicing open an eye for an extraction is a frightening procedure. Once the knife penetrates into the anterior chamber, some of the inner fluid of the eyeball starts to seep out. Then, with scissors, the edge of the cornea is sliced open halfway around. The cornea rapidly goes flat as the fluid flows out and the eye loses its shape.

Lifting up the edge of the cornea, one can see the whitened lens (cataract) through the pupil, hiding behind the iris. My magnifying loupes help me to see detail, but they also serve to emphasize the tremor of my hands. I call for the cryophake, a special tool necessary to extract the lens and to touch the cataract so that it can be removed as a frozen ball.

The cryophake? My Gabonese assistant forgot to get it! He had been up during the night and was a little tired. Up to this point I had been trying hard to be calm. Now it was even more difficult.

While putting another retraction stitch in the edge of the cornea, I noticed that I was losing control of the steadiness in my hands. Waiting for the cryophake, I could only imagine what might happen if I were unable to relax enough to suture the cornea. I couldn't leave the eye wide open! Would my assistant be able to do it? He had done a lot of suturing, but could he do this? I recalled once again the warning about "occasional cataract surgeons."

My assistant finally arrived with the instrument and the cataract tumbled out uneventfully with a gentle tug. The pupil was clear, with no bleeding, and revealed the deep blackness of the vitreous.

Now there was no time to waste. The cornea had to be closed quickly so that no vitreous would escape. My hands were still shaking with excitement and nervousness. I breathed a prayer for help from the Lord and under my breath commanded my hands to be still. Amazingly they stopped shaking long enough to get in the three sutures necessary. The eye regained its shape and the cornea was as clear as glass.

The patient hadn't yet blinked or moved. But the anesthesia was starting to wear off. Mama Christine reacted a little when the eye ointment and dressing were applied. But we had made it! There could still be complications, but the major hurdles were past. I was so grateful to God for the gift of calm at the moment I needed it. It was especially meaningful to one who has always been a somewhat reluctant surgeon. I knew better than anyone that a miracle had taken place.

Four months after her surgery, Mama Christine, wearing thick lenses given to her by the hospital, was able to walk unescorted to church for the women's conference. It was a highlight of the year for the entire village and she had much to be thankful for.

When Terry returned to the village the next week to attend a ladies' Bible study, Mama Christine arrived too—on her own. The leader asked everyone to share one thing they were thankful for during the recent conference.

Mama Christine said she remembered Rev. Fairley saying years ago that what he was doing was just the beginning, that not everything would be accomplished at once, and that in the years to come she, Mama Christine, would live to see her children become mature Christians, even teaching her.

His words had come true. It was the daughters of Mama Christine's people who had taught at the women's conference. She was thankful for what God had done in 60 years of Mission work in Gabon. "God's grandchildren" were now leading His Church.

After hearing this report, I was even more thankful for how much God had helped this hesitant surgeon. That operation was a breakthrough of sorts. Since then, by the grace of God, my subsequent cataract extractions have been generally successful.

And every Sunday, as I sit on the well-worn pews of the Bongolo church, I, too, am impressed with what has been accomplished by the faithful preaching and teaching of God's Word in Gabon.

> *"Tell it to your children, and let your children*
> *tell it to their children, and their children*
> *to the next generation."*
> Joel 1:3

# "ARE YOU HEALED?"

## MALI, WEST AFRICA —————————————

### Joan Foster

December 22nd will always be a day to remember for missionary nurse Barbara Sorensen.

The day had begun with a routine trip into San for shopping. As usual, her car was full of people and baggage. But a car loaded beyond reason is no problem to Barb. She is so used to the roads that she doesn't even take notice of rocks, potholes or dust. She just does what has to be done.

On the way home, some of the passengers wanted to stop and pick something from a tree by the side of the road. Barb, always her smiling, accommodating, agreeable self, stopped.

Since the Mali sun is very hot, she decided to stand under the shade of a nearby tree. She did not know that a pencil viper had decided to keep cool itself there as well. Barb stepped on the snake. It retaliated by biting her on the right heel.

Suddenly Barb's good day had turned to a bad one. Pain shot up her leg. She became dizzy and nauseous. Confusion and fear gripped the hearts of her passengers. What would happen to Barb? Everyone knows that a bite from a pencil viper can be fatal.

One of the passengers drove the truck home and

Barb was quickly given the anti-venom serum injection needed to counteract the poison that was by now spreading throughout her body.

People began to pray—and wait. What would happen to their Sanmuhan (God's gift)? The missionary family also united their hearts in prayer for their colleague and friend.

Six days went by and Barb was not getting better. She still had a lot of bleeding and felt extremely weak from the loss of blood.

Our field medical personnel were meeting in a nearby city for a three-day spiritual retreat. Barb should have been there with us. We missed her and prayed for a quick recovery.

Thursday morning we received word that Barb was still not improving. The loss of blood was not decreasing. Hearing the news, we stopped what we were doing and had special prayer for Barb's healing.

I left a note at the Mission to be relayed to her the next morning on the radio. The note read, "Barb, we had special prayer for you today. Are you healed?"

Before the message could be radioed the next morning, Barbara announced to all our missionary family that she had felt healing take place in her body at the very time we prayed for her.

What a time of rejoicing that was for us. And what an encouragement to our faith as we once again realized that God is not only our Savior, our Sanctifier, our Coming King, but our Healer as well. Praise His Name!

*"I am the LORD, who heals you."*
Exodus 15:26

# THE INCREDIBLE JOURNEY

## PHILIPPINE ISLANDS
## VIETNAM, SOUTHEAST ASIA——

### Jean Livingston

"**H**e is dead! My son is dead!" Mother Thao wanted to wail aloud. But even the emotional relief which comes with tears was denied her. She must keep absolutely silent!

Little Vu had become violently seasick on the first day of the typhoon. The storm raged on, showing no sign of mercy. Wave after wave pounded across the small boat. The desperate refugees clung to one another and cried to the gods of their ancestors.

It had been four days since Vu had eaten anything and on the fourth day he had become too weak to move. Finally, with one last look into the face of his mother, Vu closed his eyes and breathed no more.

Still, Thao clutched the body of her lifeless son and once again repeated: "When you pass through the waters, I will be with you; and when you pass through the rivers, they will not sweep over you. When you walk through the fire, you will not be burned; the flames will not set you ablaze. . . . Fear not, for I have redeemed you; I have summoned you by name; you are mine" (Isaiah 43:2, 1).

Nguyen Thi Phuong Thao knew that there would be many risks when she decided to flee Vietnam. Her husband had successfuly escaped the yoke of communism six years before and was waiting for her and their two sons, Vu and Dung, ages 10 and 12, in California.

Thao had paid for this trip with everything she owned. On her finger was one gold ring, her last possession of value, which she would use to ransom her life or the lives of her sons should Thai pirates attack the boat.

The eight-hour bus trip from Saigon would land the refugees at a secluded beach on the South China Sea far removed from the eyes of the dreaded communist shore patrol. The midnight rendezvous on the beach called for meticulous calculation. Every detail of the trip was timed almost to the minute.

The bus was making good time; in fact, it was ahead of schedule. Therefore, the bus driver, himself a well-paid collaborator in the escape business, cleverly made several stops to "repair" the "broken" vehicle.

Shortly after midnight the bus arrived at the beach exactly as planned.

"Everyone silent!" commanded the bus driver. Grabbing their meager possessions, the frightened passengers quietly transferred to several small row boats which would take them out beyond the breakers to where a larger vessel was waiting.

Suddenly everyone began to scream: "Wait! Wait! Don't leave us! We are coming!" The shadowy hulk of the ship, its motor already started, had turned its bow eastward in the direction of

the open sea which would eventually take all on
board to Morong Beach, Luzon, Philippines.

Finally Thao, her boys and the rest of the passengers managed to scramble on board for the incredible journey.

The first day at sea was quiet except for the
drone of the engine and the splashing of water
against the sides of the boat. But no one was prepared for the news.

"The boat captain is not on board," the helmsman said. "He has fled with the gold! I have no
idea how to steer this boat to the Philippines. We
should turn back!"

"No! Absolutely not!" chanted the 120 angry
passengers. And so, despite the risks of an inexpe-
rienced helmsman, all the passengers pressed for
immediate continuation of the journey.

On the second day, the wind increased until
an unexpected typhoon struck with all its fury,
sending down unending torrents of rain. The
wind-whipped boat tossed about in the churning
sea like some plastic toy. The refugees tied
themselves to one another and to the side of the
boat.

All the rice and what little food they had was
now soaked with sea water. There was no pure
water to drink. The raging sea contaminated
everything it touched. For four days it seemed
that they were locked in the jaws of death itself.

The inevitable result was illness for many, including little Vu, who finally succumbed. Mother
Thao was gripped with fear. The Vietnamese people are at times very superstitious. If the other
passengers knew that Vu was dead, they would
consider this a bad omen. For fear of retaliation

by evil spirits they would insist on tossing her son's body into the sea.

Noticing that the child had not stirred in a long time, a few of the women crammed in next to the mother and started to massage the stiffened arms and legs of the boy. After about 20 minutes of this age-old Asian practice, Vu's eyelids quivered and he began to stir.

"He's alive again! He's alive!" Mother Thao now wept openly, but this time it was with tears of joy. A mother's silent prayer had been heard above the roar of the angry waves.

On the sixth day, the sea was calm except for the never-ending ocean swells which lifted and lowered the boat again and again. By now the ship's fuel supply was totally exhausted and for one night they drifted, not knowing what fate this turn of events might bring.

Suddenly a large white freighter was sighted. Everyone shouted frantically in an effort to flag down the approaching vessel. But the cries of the refugees soon turned into forlorn wailing as the freighter, only 20 meters away, deliberately passed them by. Despair gripped their hearts like some angry sea serpent.

"Mama, why didn't God hear our prayers and cause that freighter to stop and take us aboard? Why, Mama, why?" sobbed Vu. How could this mother satisfy her son's bewildered heart when she herself did not know the answer to his question?

"Why?" Mother Thao began hestitantly. "God *has* answered our prayers, my son. Did He not shield us from the eyes of the enemy along the highway? Did he not keep us afloat during the terrible typhoon? Did He not deliver you from death and raise you back to life again? We shall continue to believe God. You pray, Vu. You pray!"

The two little brothers, drenched with sea water, hungry and weak almost beyond endurance, bowed their heads and began to pray—just two little Vietnamese boys bravely obeying the instruction of their mother with simple faith.

Fifteen minutes later the faint outline of another ship was spotted on the horizon. Slowly it approached until even the faces of the men on deck became visible.

"They see us! They are going to save us!" cried the refugees.

The ship circled the refugee boat once in an attempt to slow speed and stop. And stop it did! A long rope ladder was lowered, but the Vietnamese found they were hardly able to stand, their legs being in a state of contracture from days in cramped positions. Yet, one by one, they struggled and strained. Strength from some unknown Source was added to theirs and up the ladder they climbed. Thao and her two precious sons were also lifted on board the Greek freighter.

"Mama," little Vu said, smiling into the strained face of his mother. "Mama, God heard *my* prayer, didn't He? I prayed and God sent us this ship, huh, Mama, huh?"

"Yes, little one. God heard your prayer. God has heard all our prayers. Indeed He has rescued us not once but several times on this incredible journey. When we passed through the waters He kept His promise. He was with us!"

*"Fear not, for I have redeemed you; I have summoned you by name; you are mine. When you pass through the waters, I will be with you. . . ."*
Isaiah 43:1-2

# THE
# HIDING PLACE

## ECUADOR, SOUTH AMERICA

### Stephanie Beers

The snow-capped volcanoes were breathtaking, the temperature chilly, yet comfortable, the rustic surroundings of the hotel inviting. Having lived in Ecuador for only six months, I really didn't know what to expect my first time at the field forum.

The first few days away from Quito, about two hours away, proved to be refreshing, the messages challenging—just what we needed as we settled in to serve the Lord in a new culture.

Then, suddenly, on the next to the last afternoon of our stay I began to feel nauseous. I had recently begun taking medicine for amoebas. *No doubt that's making me sick,* I thought stoically to myself.

However, the nausea quickly escalated into pain comparable to childbirth. I tried desperately to vomit, thinking it would ease my discomfort. I was alternately sweating, shivering and writhing in my bed. Several missionaries came to pray with me. The pain subsided sufficiently to allow me to breathe easier. I was grateful for that small mercy but it was evident that something was seriously wrong.

I was given two options—ride back to Quito over bumpy, curvy roads, or go to the nearest town, about 20 minutes away, and look for a doctor. It had already been determined that there was no doctor in this beautiful little mountain village.

I chose to go to the nearby town. I was loaded into a waiting van and off we went in search of a clinic that was open on a Saturday afternoon.

The first clinic we saw was *Clinica Dolorosa* (Painful Clinic). It was open. But with a name like that, I wasn't sure I was happy to be there!

By the time the doctor examined me, my blood pressure was incredibly low. The room was spinning. He asked me questions about my family including whether anyone had ever had gallbladder problems. I told him that my grandmother, my mother, my aunt and my sister had all had their gallbladders removed. He recommended that I have mine checked as soon as I returned to Quito. He gave me an injection of something. What, I didn't know, but by that time I didn't really care.

Two days after returning to Quito I met with a surgeon. The sonogram informed us that I should soon be added to the list of gallbladderless females in my family.

The surgery was scheduled for the following week. My husband, Bruce, and I prayed for the Lord's protection and guidance throughout the operation. With fear and trembling I was admitted to the hospital. *Why does this have to happen to me in this foreign land?* I wondered to myself and to God. But by the time I was wheeled into the operating room a deep peace had invaded my heart and mind. Within a few hours I was back in my room.

I gripped Bruce's hand as wave after wave of pain rippled through me. In response to my questions, the nurses reminded me that I had a catheter in my back that was constantly dripping pain medicine directly into the incision site. I certainly did not want to be a complainer, so I did my best to keep quiet.

By the following morning the pain was almost unbearable, radiating in excruciating waves from my abdomen to my shoulder. I was also having trouble breathing.

An X-ray confirmed the doctor's suspicion— while inserting the catheter in my back, my lung had been punctured. Air had been slowly leaking out and was now trapped between my lung and the lining of my lung, a condition technically known as pleural effusion. I also had not received any pain medicine since the surgery!

The doctor asked Bruce to leave the room. Before he even reached the door, the doctor's knife had already sliced a gaping hole in my side. I could see the nurse fumbling to put the doctor's glasses on his face as he explained that he was twisting the forceps into the hole he had just cut in my side and was forcing them through my rib cage in order to make way for the chest tube that he was about to insert. The trapped air needed to be removed, he said, and this was the only way to do it.

Finally, as he assured me that the worst was over, he inserted the other end of the tube into a huge bottle of water. Together we watched the bubbles rise to the surface, an indicator that the trapped air was being released. At least something was working! An oxygen mask was strapped on me and I was quickly wheeled to another room.

There, a lung specialist reversed the suction and my lung re-inflated. I was given a pain shot and everybody went home except Connie, a missionary colleague and friend who had volunteered to spend the night with me.

I soon drifted off to sleep.

Around midnight I was awakened by an uncomfortable feeling of pressure in my chest. I asked Connie to pray with me and to read from the Psalms. *Psalm 23 would be very appropriate about now,* I thought to myself. The pain began to return. My breathing was becoming more labored. I asked her to sing some worship choruses.

In response to a question about my increasing discomfort, the nurse on duty informed us that there was nobody in respiratory therapy during the night, that I was not due to have any more pain medicine for several hours and that my doctor would be in to check on me in the morning. By then, I was convinced that I wouldn't be around in the morning for him to check on.

As the night wore on I began to gurgle when I breathed. On closer inspection, Connie and I realized that the water in that huge jug was coming up the tube and draining directly into my lung! I felt like I was drowning. I had only one good lung (as good as any lung can be in the high Andean altitude) and the recently re-inflated one was quickly taking on water.

Exhausted from the Psalm reading and chorus singing, Connie finally asked the Lord to wake up somebody to pray for us. I certainly needed divine intervention and so did she. It had been a long night. Mercifully, the nurse came in and gave me a shot.

The first rays of pink were streaking the eastern sky as I closed my eyes. Echoing in my mind were the words of Psalm 32:7 "You are my hiding place; you will protect me from trouble and surround me with songs of deliverance."

After what seemed like only minutes I was awakened by the doctor. He said he needed to remove the tube. When I asked how he was going to do that, he said, "Like this." Putting one foot on the side of the bed, he leaned back and gave a yank. I saw stars.

"I hope your body will re-absorb the remaining fluid," he said as he sutured the hole shut.

A few weeks later, I received a letter from a woman who to this day I have never met. She had picked up one of our prayer cards at a women's retreat.

In the middle of that night she had awakened to pray for her father who was having open heart surgery. As she opened her Bible to read and pray for him, our prayer card fell out. The Lord prompted her to pray for the young woman whose picture was on the card. She wrote to ask if I had had a special need on that day at that time.

Indeed, I had!

Buoyed by the direct evidence of the Lord's intervention in my body, I went for my post-surgery check-up. Even as we drove in the car, I was still gurgling. But, in the office, as I inhaled for yet another chest X-ray, I felt a pop. What followed was the deepest, most wonderful breath I have ever taken. I was given a clean bill of health.

Praise the Lord!

*"We do not want you to be uninformed, brothers,*
*about the hardships we suffered . . . far beyond*
*our ability to endure, so that we despaired even of life.*
*Indeed, in our hearts we felt the sentence of death.*
*But this happened that we might not rely on*
*ourselves but on God. . . . He has delivered us . . .*
*and he will deliver us. On him we have set our hope*
*that he will continue to deliver us, as you help us by*
*your prayers. Then many will give thanks*
*on our behalf for the gracious favor granted us in*
*answer to the prayers of many."*
2 Corinthians 1:8-11

# HEALED!

## ISREAL

### Virginia Jacober

My suitcase was almost packed as I prepared to leave for the Holy Land. I had been invited to help at a conference center a few miles south of Bethlehem. It would be wonderful to see dear Arab friends again and to visit my Bedouin friends in the desert. What a great privilege this would be to serve the Lord even though I was an officially retired missionary.

After more than 40 years of traveling to and from India and Israel, I'd had a lot of experience with suitcases and had learned how to pack every nook and cranny full. No space was wasted.

This occasion was no exception. The problem was that, after I had crammed everything possible into the two cases, I could not lift them off the bed! So I slid them down to the floor and dragged them to the door.

But the damage had been done.

By the time I boarded the plane I had a terrible backache which persisted and increased when I lifted the suitcases off the carousel and onto a luggage cart to change planes. The repetition of this procedure in Vienna and again in Tel Aviv only added to the discomfort.

I arrived at the conference center full of joy at the prospect of serving the Lord as a volunteer. The missionaries welcomed me warmly and showed me to a nice apartment on the second floor. With negotiating a flight of steps obviously to become part of my daily routine, I prayed desperately for healing.

One of my assignments was to teach English to Muslims from a nearby refugee camp. I loved the young men and women. They were anxious to learn and they came faithfully. But soon opposition erupted because I was using the Gospel of John as a text. A threatening letter was fastened to the gate of the compound. Dire consequences, it said, would befall any who came to learn English, as well as the missionaries.

Classes were cancelled.

After a week or so, however, one young man surreptitiously appeared at the door, out of breath, to say he wanted to continue studying. Every day he came faithfully at various times and from different directions. I could only pray that God's Word would penetrate his heart.

In the four years since I had been in Israel, the presence of Israeli security had escalated along with the fighting. More Jewish soldiers patrolled the streets of Jerusalem and West Bank towns. Numerous road blocks continued to exasperate Arab travelers. Day and night I could hear guns being fired in the nearby field as the army trained new recruits to defend their land.

The problem was that the Arabs believe it is their land, too. They have lived there for centuries. Frustration and heartache over losses in property and the death of loved ones stabbed my heart. I felt their pain. I suffered with them.

My prayers for personal healing did not seem to be effective. I wondered why. Was my faith not strong enough? I knew the Lord could heal miraculously or by means of medical help because He had done both for me in the past. But this time there seemed to be no answer.

Riding rickety buses into Bethlehem did not help to ease the discomfort. But I loved seeing heather blooming on the hillsides and donkeys carrying loads of vegetables into the market. I visited a young Muslim woman who had been my neighbor. She always called me "Mother" and we loved each other very much. Had she made a commitment to Christ? She did not tell me. But I gave her a Bible.

I rode out into the Judean desert to visit Bedouin friends and drank the traditional strong Turkish coffee in demitasse cups. Their way of life had not changed. Goats and chickens and children roamed in and out of the tent. Sheep grazed on the stony hillside and tethered donkeys brayed their complaints.

As I lowered myself to the ground inside the tent for the first time in 15 years, sharp pain jagged through my back. The visit was all too brief and I left reluctantly, knowing I might never see these dear friends again. My only hope was that we would meet some day in heaven.

One night I awoke about 3 o'clock. As I got out of bed, I suddenly realized there was no pain! I was healed! How could this be? I thanked the Lord and with great relief went back to sleep.

The next morning I understood. The middle of the night in Israel was Wednesday evening in the

United States. The prayer service was in progress at Hillside Chapel, my church in Dayton, Ohio. Someone had prayed for me! The pain had disappeared.

It never returned.

> *"Praise the LORD, O my soul,*
> *and forget not all his benefits—*
> *who forgives all your sins*
> *and heals all your diseases."*
> Psalm 103:2-3

# THE HIGH GOD'S HIPPOS

## GABON, West Africa

### David C. Thompson, MD

The hippopotamus is the most unlikely killer in West Africa, but there is no doubt that hippos can and do occasionally kill humans.

The people of Gabon fear the hippos as much or more than they fear the crocodile. Hippopotami are nocturnal, preferring to come out of the water at night to graze along the shores. Although they weigh from two to four tons, they are surprisingly agile on land and, for a short distance, can outrun a man. They have acute night vision, a good sense of smell and very sensitive hearing.

During the day they remain hidden in rivers, ponds, lakes or swamps, walking on the bottom to forage for food or hiding in mud by submerging themselves completely, leaving only their nostrils exposed.

Although hippos are air-breathers, they can hold their breath underwater for up to five minutes. When they need air, they swim to the surface and, exposing only their nostrils, refill their lungs before returning to the bottom.

Man is probably the hippo's greatest enemy. Africans have hunted hippos for years, using spears, harpoons and, more recently, guns. If a hunter shoots a hippo in the water, he sometimes must wait six to eight hours for the body to float to the surface.

A hippo will demonstratate its hostility by opening its huge mouth, revealing its tusks and teeth and snarling. On other occasions, it will simply surface without warning and, opening its hinged jaws, seize a canoe in its huge mouth and either overturn it or break it.

The best way to escape a hippo is to dive deep and swim underwater as far as possible before surfacing quietly. If a splashing victim is within reach, the hippo may seize a leg or even a torso in its powerful jaws, crushing bones and soft tissue. If the victim continues to show signs of life, the hippo may drag him to the bottom until he drowns.

At our hospital in Bongolo one day I talked with a man named Philippe. I asked him if he was certain he would go to heaven when he died. He answered that he thought he would. When I asked him why, he recounted the following story.

For many years Philippe had worked for an oil exploration company in the great swamps that drained into the Ogoue River. One day his company ordered him to move with his family to another drilling location in the swamp. The company promised to send an outboard-powered canoe to Lambarene to move them. The trip would take about four hours.

Philippe and his wife packed up their few belongings and got their three children, aged three months to eight years, ready to go. The boat was supposed to pick them up at 10 a.m., but when the family arrived, the pilot and his helper told them to wait while they went to a nearby bar for refreshments.

Two hours later Philippe went looking for the men. They were so drunk they could hardly stand. They reluctantly agreed to return to the canoe.

The men were sober enough to operate the boat, but now they were already three hours late. An hour into the trip, they made a wrong turn. Another hour passed before they discovered their mistake and turned around. By the time they got back on course, night was fast approaching.

As the darkness settled, large numbers of huge, fish-eating bats swooped past the canoe, skimming above the water and seizing the fish feeding near the surface. By this time even the boatmen were uneasy, but they assured Philippe and his wife that they knew the way so well they could continue in the dark.

The vessel was motoring through the middle of a vast, shallow, tea-colored swamp when suddenly the motor sputtered and died. They were out of gas.

It was a moonless night. In the inky darkness they were unable to find a suitable place to step ashore and build a fire. What looked like dry land turned out to be sinking mud covered with plants. There was nothing to do but remain all night in the canoe.

About midnight they were awakened by a strange sound. It began as a gentle splash, followed by a snort and the sound of air being expelled from a very large animal. Something had surfaced about 20 feet away. The ripples in the water rocked the canoe. Soon other animals joined the first, followed by more. Sounds of heavy breathing and splashing were all around them.

By now the adults in the boat were wide awake, trying to control their fear. The animals around them were hippos. They did not seem to be aware of the humans floating quietly in the darkness only a few feet away.

As the passengers drifted in breathless silence, hordes of mosquitos descended on them. Philippe and his wife covered the children with cloths and, as soundlessly as they could, tried to cover themselves, but there were not enough towels to go around. Their arms and legs were soon covered with angry bites but they dared not slap the mosquitos for fear of startling the hippos.

*Surely,* thought Philippe, these animals will smell us. And if they smell us and become frightened, they will attack our canoe.

As fear clutched at his heart, Philippe thought about his three children. *What if the baby cries? What if one of the children whimpers in his sleep?* He dared not even whisper a warning to his wife. He knew she understood the danger as much as he.

As the huge beasts splashed round him in the darkness, Philippe, for the first time in his life thought seriously about the "High God," the "God of thunder and lightning," the "God who had created all life." He had been told as a child that the High God cared nothing about men. But as the hippos grazed in the swamp around them and the tension in the canoe rose, Philippe began to wonder if the High God would hear him if he prayed.

*Why should He hear me,* he thought. *I don't have anything to offer Him.*

As the minutes dragged into hours and the silent terror grew, Philippe became desperate. Without any idea of why it would help or how he should do it, he began to pray silently to the High God. He asked Him to keep the hippos from becoming frightened and attacking them. He promised the High God that if He would save them, he, Philippe, would do whatever He wanted. Since he could offer God nothing, he appealed for mercy.

It was the longest night of their lives. The hours dragged on endlessly as the hippos fed and played around them.

About 3 a.m., exhausted by the intensity of the situation, Philippe finally dozed off. When he awoke, the sun was coming up. The hippos had left sometime during the night without even bothering the boat or its occupants. Several hours later, another company boat came looking for the traders and towed them to their destination.

Several years later Philippe's company offered him a hefty bonus if he would retire early. He accepted the offer and settled in his wife's village in south Gabon. Within a week of his arrival, he met a man from the village who was called "pastor." The man's French was very poor. So Philippe did not think he knew much. Nevertheless, he agreed to visit the pastor's church the next Sunday.

The service lasted about two hours. Philippe was fascinated with what the pastor had to say. He read from a Book in which he claimed the High God spoke to men. He said the High God had a Son named Jesus who had lived on the earth. Could this be the same High God who had answered his prayer? Where had the Book come from and how could this ignorant pastor know the High God?

After several weeks Philippe paid the pastor a visit. He learned that a white man had brought the Book to south Gabon years before and had taught the pastor about the High God and His Son Jesus. The white man had also translated the High God's Book into the language of the village.

Phillipe was astonished beyond words. He had met and worked for quite a few white men. None of them seemed to know anything about the High God. In fact, they were so ignorant they didn't even know the spirits were real! How could people so ignorant about spiritual things know about the High God?

The words in the High God's Book finally convinced Philippe. He had never heard anything like it before. Everything the Book said about people, about himself and about the world was true. He was amazed when he heard how the High God loved the people of the world so much that He sent His Son Jesus to earth to die in their place. It all began to make sense. The reason the High God had heard his prayer and had saved his family from the hippos was because He loved them!

"Because of the hippos," he concluded, "I found Jesus. Now I know I will go to heaven when I die." Philippe had been saved by the High God's hippos!

*"For God so loved the world that he gave his one and only Son, that whoever believes in him shall not perish but have eternal life."*
John 3:16

# GOD IS THE HEALER

## Dwayne Buhler

As my wife Rhonda and I left for Brazil there were many uncertainties and unanswered questions. Would we be able to learn Portuguese? Would we be able to fit in? What did the Lord have in store for us? And one question that weighed heavily upon us: Would the medical facilities in Brazil be adequate just in case something happened?

Rhonda had been born with a disease known as hydrocephalus—water on the brain. The natural drainage system that removes fluid from the brain was blocked at birth causing increasing pressure and pain. Five weeks after her birth, Rhonda's mother noticed that her head was increasing in size and took her to the hospital for a checkup. Her parents anxiously watched and prayed as the surgeon performed the delicate shunt-valve operation.

The surgery was successful. However, at 18 months, a second surgery was performed. And Rhonda grew and developed as any other child. In fact, she surpassed all expectations.

During Rhonda's growing up years her mother often reminded her that God had a very special purpose for her life. But at 12 years of age, she began to experience severe headaches, then nausea, and eventually loss of coordination. She was to be evacuated to a hospital 700 miles away. But before she left, the pastor and his wife came to pray for her healing. It was a simple prayer that God would touch and heal this young girl.

Her parents watched in amazement as the symptoms reversed themselves and Rhonda was restored to complete health.

Part of the process for our final departure to Brazil was to obtain medical clearance, especially as it related to Rhonda's childhood surgeries. We were overjoyed to hear that everything was functioning normally and that the problem would not be a deterrent to overseas ministry.

During our first three years of service we completed Portuguese language study, our two children were born and we were integrated into a church-planting team in the large southern city of Porto Alegre, Brazil. The Lord had been so very good to us.

Then came September 1993. We had just come through an extremely heavy month of ministry involvements. So we planned a short mid-week vacation at a retreat center in the mountains. The plan was to rest and spend time alone with the children. However, that was not to be.

Rhonda began to experience severe headaches—migraine headaches. They would come and go, but they always returned with increased intensity. At first we thought they were due to the stress of the heavy load we had been carrying. But the headaches persisted. Finally, the pain was so severe that Rhonda could not bend over to pick our young son out of his crib.

We asked people to pray for God's intervention in Rhonda's life. And we began to search for a neurosurgeon. The doctor who had delivered our son gave us the names of three qualified doctors, but suggested that we first try to get in contact with Dr. Nilo Lopes.

"If I were you," he said simply, "I would go to Dr. Lopes. He's the best."

Dr. Lopes was a pleasant man, his broad smile reassuring as he began to ask us in Portuguese about the nature of the problem. We had barely begun to explain when Dr. Lopes broke into perfect English and asked two seemingly irrelevant questions.

"Rhonda," he asked, "in what year were you born?"

Rhonda began to answer in Portuguese, then corrected herself. "Well, in 1964."

"And in what city were you born?" probed Dr. Lopes further.

"In Vancouver, Canada," responded Rhonda.

Dr. Lopes leaned forward on his desk.

"Then your doctor was Dr. Peter Moyes, wasn't he?"

Rhonda could only stare in amazement. "Why, yes he was. How do you know?"

Dr. Lopes went on to explain that at the time of Rhonda's birth there were two surgeons who were leaders in shunt-valve research and technology. One was Dr. Moyes at the Vancouver General Hospital. The other one was from Chicago. Dr. Lopes had been studying in Chicago at the time. He knew exactly what type of valve had been used. And he was able to relieve the pressure Rhonda was experiencing.

After further testing, Dr. Lopes explained that the old valve and tubing had become blocked and it must either be unclogged or replaced. He gave us the option of returning to Canada for the surgery or of allowing him to operate there in Porto Alegre. Either way, the surgery would have to be done within the next few days.

Rhonda's valve was replaced by Dr. Lopes on October 23, 1993. While she was in the recovery room, he sat down with me for a cup of coffee and jokingly assured me that with current advances in technology he could give a 50-year guarantee for "parts and labor."

Rhonda has since returned to the "normal" life of being a missionary, a wife and the mother of two small children. We give the glory to the Lord, for as Dr. Lopes said, "God is the Healer; the surgeon is only His instrument."

> *"If the LORD delights in a man's way,*
> *he makes his steps firm; though he stumble,*
> *he will not fall, for the LORD*
> *upholds him with his hand."*
> Psalm 37: 23-24

# I CAN?

**MALI, West Africa**————————————

## Marsha Barnwell

Philippians 4:13 is one of those verses that Christians often quote, especially when they are confronting difficult circumstances in their lives.

As a missionary, I have repeatedly reminded myself of that verse.

"I can do all things through Christ which strengtheneth me," I quietly whispered to myself when tears rolled down my cheeks as I said those first goodbyes to our family and friends and headed to France for language study.

"I can do all things through Christ . . . ," I repeated as I stumbled through French language study and then again through Bambara language study.

"I can do all things through Christ . . . ," I reminded the Lord and myself as I watched my children go away to boarding school. That verse was always an encouragement to keep going, to remember that with God's help I could handle whatever came my way.

However, one day during our second term, that verse became an even greater challenge to me as God stretched my faith a little farther.

We had just spent two days away from our station attending the monthly district pastors' meeting. The fellowship had been good, the news of district ministries encouraging.

As usual, the meeting had gone all night and Randy, my husband, was very tired. I had sat up late with the women of the church, so I was tired, too. We were looking forward to getting back home and getting some rest.

But God had other plans.

We loaded up our vehicle with the pastors who lived near us and headed for home. As we dropped the men off at the local church compound, the pastor's wife said, "Come and see the sick men who came in from the bush yesterday."

We were not prepared for the sight that met our eyes. There, lying on grass mats in the mud-brick guesthouse, were three men, all burned beyond recognition. We did not know any of them—or so we thought.

As it turned out, just the week before, Randy and I had visited their village and had eaten our noon meal with them and their families. As their story unfolded, our hearts were filled with a deep compassion for these suffering believers.

It seems that while their pastor was away at the meeting, a new believer came to the church and wanted to burn his fetishes. Since the pastor was not there to do it, the elder of the church, his son and his son-in-law decided to perform the task.

As was the custom, they took the fetishes outside the village and built a fire. There are many different kinds of fetishes in Mali. The witch doctor makes them out of different objects—teeth from an animal, bird feathers, dog hair. Some-

times bits of gold are put into the fetish and sometimes gun powder. Experienced pastors make it a
practice to open up each fetish to check the con-
tents before throwing it into the fire.

Unfortunately, on that fateful day, with the pastor away, the elder forgot to open the fetishes.
They contained gun powder and, when they hit
the fire, they blew up in the faces of the three
men.

The old man was standing up when the blast
from the fire hit him in the face and chest. All his
hair was singed off. One of the younger men was
leaning over the fire. His face, chest and arms
were all burned. The worst of the three was the
youngest man. He had stooped close to the fire
and received the full blast of the explosion on the
front of his body. Third degree burns covered his
legs, arms, face and chest.

By the time we saw the men, they had come on
the back of motorbikes from their village to the
medical clinic in our town. They had received
treatment at the clinic and their open sores had
been wrapped in bandages. The biggest fear of
each of them was that they would be permanently
blind.

The next day we went back to visit the men.
Tears filled my eyes as I witnessed their agony.
They had just come back from the clinic where
the local pastor reported that the bandages had
been literally ripped off with no compassion or
pity. At that moment, I determined that I would
do all I could to help them. That meant taking
over the treatment they needed.

I am not a nurse but, beginning that day, God
taught me the truth of Philippians 4:13. I was

about to find out that I could do all things through Him Who would give me strength. I leaned heavily on that strength during the weeks that followed.

We worked in an area that did not have a Mission-run clinic. But our nurses from other areas had given us some medicines they had received from the States. That medicine included several large jars of burn salve. And thanks to our women's groups back in America, we were also well-equipped with rolled bandages.

Each morning I went down to the church and began the long process of wetting down the bandages, taking off the old ones as gently as I could, cleaning the sores and then putting medicine on them and re-wrapping them. By the time I was finished with the third man, my back was aching from leaning over the mats and I was both physically and emotionally drained.

Several days into the routine, the men began to cough up black mucous from their lungs. We realized then that they had also been injured internally. Once again God gave me wisdom and I began to make powdered milk for them to drink.

Each day as I dressed their wounds I knew I was hurting them because of the nature of their burns. Tears ran down my face until one day something changed—God led me to sing. From then on, I sang to the men as I worked. It helped them to relax and all of us to laugh amidst the pain.

As they began to heal I had the task of cutting away the rotting skin. That was probably the most difficult thing I faced. It was only through God's strength and His compassion that I was able to persist.

From the time the men were burned, word was sent throughout Mali for Christians to pray. The fetish worshipers were claiming that the power of the fetish had caused the accident. But as the Christians prayed, God worked.

Two weeks after the mishap, the men were able to go back to their village. Their bodies were already beginning to heal and I taught their wives how to change the bandages. No one's eyes were permanently injured by the blast.

Several months after they returned home, we saw the youngest man who had been the most severely burned. I had cut the skin off his entire hand and yet now there was only one small pink spot that witnessed to his accident. Eventually all of the men were completely healed. None of them have any scars. God had performed a miracle.

> *"I can do everything through him*
> *who gives me strength."*
> Philippians 4:13

# GOD'S MULE

## COLOMBIA, SOUTH AMERICA————

### Helen Constance

Upon a dangerous Andes trail
I lurch ahead and swish my tail;
   I'm just a mule.
They pile a load upon my back
And on each side they hang a sack
   Like I'm a fool!

Then up the trail I groan and grieve,
I lurch and sweat and pull and heave.
   I'm just a mule.
Through sun and rain in heat or cold
Nobody cares that I am old;
   I sweat and drool.

Sometimes I stop—I've had enough.
They beat me and they treat me rough
   'cause I'm a mule.
They say I'm stubborn, dumb and mean
But I am smarter than I seem
   And I'm no fool.

A missionary rides ahead
And holds the rope by which is led
   His poor, dumb mule!
While I must struggle with the weight

Of Bibles, hymnbooks . . . and my fate
  'cause I'm a mule.

At trail's end all the people gather
But no one notices the lather
  Of a mule.
They hug the preacher, buy his books
Feed him well—but no one looks
  At a mule.

Until at last they think to feed me
And send somebody out to lead me
  Beside a pool.
I hear the sermon and the singing
From hymnbooks, but . . . who did the bringing?
  'twas I, the mule.

I'm God's creation and He needs me
To carry loads where'er He leads me;
  I am His tool.
I'm stubborn, ugly and dumb, they say
But this one thing's my only pay . . .
  I am *His* mule.

# A CRIB AND A SHAKER

## ZAIRE/CONGO, AFRICA

### Myra Brown

On a cold, dark Friday night during our first furlough, God gave us our first child, Bethany. We had waited many years to see her little form and were overwhelmed by the miracle of her arrival. She was just four days old when she came into our hearts and home.

For the next six months my whole world revolved around this amazing baby. Yet in the back of my mind I knew our return to Zaire was fast approaching. I had every intention of returning, but somehow I couldn't imagine transferring child care from Canada with its every comfort, every baby product, every service, every security, to Zaire with all its challenges.

What if Bethany got sick? Where could I buy more soya formula if I ran out? Would I have enough hot water to keep her clothes clean and sanitary? Although I knew in my head that millions of babies survive in Zaire and mine would, too, I felt uncomfortable leaving the easy and safe way of caring for this little wonder.

One day the mail arrived containing a letter from the late Jane Raffloer, field director for Zaire. She closed her letter by saying, "I was at Maduda this weekend and ordered Bethany's crib. It will be ready when you arrive."

I felt a warm peace flood over me. Zaire was where we belonged. After all, Bethany's crib was waiting. Somehow that one piece of furniture symbolized the total package which would be necessary to care for our child in Zaire. From that moment on, I had peace of mind as we prepared to leave.

Eleven years later a parallel scenario unfolded. Following two terms in Zaire and a leave of absence for three years, God was taking our family back to Africa, this time to Congo.

While preparing to go, I was overwhelmed with grief. Our three years with aging parents and our large extended families, the warm church to which we belonged, the lovely house we had purchased, the freedom to study, our interesting jobs—all these things were changing. Leaving them loomed like dreadful minuses on my horizon.

Despite the Congo missionary team's warm welcome and the fascinating work waiting to be done with the churches there, I felt paralyzed with grief and deep emotional pain as we arrived in Brazzaville.

We started to attend a church which had just been planted. Meeting outside, sitting on backless planks supported by stones, I watched Bethany become reacquainted with African worship and ways. She nudged me that first Sunday when the women accompanied the singing with their metal "shakers." I smiled, remembering that her favorite toy as a baby had been one of those rattles.

One morning during that painful period of my life, a knock on the door signaled the arrival of the head deacon of the church. Mavungu shook my hand and then gave me a brand new, shiny-metal shaker! I looked at him in amazement.

"The women at the church sent this for your oldest daughter," explained the deacon.

I stammered a word of thanks and gazed wide-eyed at the gift in my hand. How did those women know a shaker held special significance to Bethany? Why had they chosen to give it to her and not to me? Why had they given it to her and not to our other daughter?

I viewed the gift of that shaker as a sign, a miracle. I felt God was telling me, "This is where you belong. This is where your family belongs. I know your past and I'm here with you now in Congo." From that time on my grief started to subside and with it the pain I was experiencing.

A crib and a shaker—God's unique instruments of comfort.

*"Praise be to the God and Father of our Lord Jesus Christ, the Father of compassion and the God of all comfort, who comforts us in all our troubles, so that we can comfort those in any trouble with the comfort we ourselves have received from God."*
2 Corinthians 1:3-4

# THE RIGHT PEOPLE IN THE RIGHT PLACES

**COLOMBIA, SOUTH AMERICA** ————

### Betty Knopp

The annual women's retreat in Colombia had long been a highlight of the year as women traveled from far and wide to fellowship together. No one was able to hide the thrill of being there to meet old friends and to make new ones.

One morning I found myself in the breakfast line in front of a lady I had not met before. I introduced myself and learned that her name was Rosa and that she came from Tolima, an area in Colombia that had in the past endured great persecution from the state church. Now, however, many large and strong evangelical churches dotted the countryside.

After a brief conversation, I asked my usual question, *"Cómo llegó a conocer el evangelio?* (How did you come to know the gospel?)"

"Do you really want to know?" Rosa responded.

"Yes, I really do," I said.

As we ate breakfast together, Rosa told me how, when she was very young, her parents had arranged her marriage to an older man. Parents in those days were more concerned for the daily material provisions of shelter, food and clothes for their daughters than to allow them to choose a life partner who could not provide for them.

Though Rosa did not feel love for her husband in the beginning, she learned to love him. He was a good man, a good husband, a good father and, of course, a good provider. He also owned a small *finca* (farm) and was well-known throughout the area.

Rosa already had 14 children and she was expecting another!

I studied her countenance. She was very pretty, well groomed, with an outward dignity and an inner peace that shone through as she spoke. I was impressed by her appearance and would be even more impressed with her testimony.

Living in the country isolated the family from social activities but periodically there were events to which they were invited. Usually liquor was served and her husband always joined others in partaking. Arguments and disagreements would often ensue, sometimes with serious consequences.

On one occasion, when Rosa's mother was visiting, Rosa asked that she be allowed to not attend a wedding. Her husband agreed and he went alone.

At the wedding the men soon got into an argument. One man took out a gun and shot Rosa's husband and his brother. Fortunately, the wounds were not fatal. Within hours he was back home from the clinic with orders to rest for a couple of weeks.

"Rosa!" her husband shouted one day as she was preparing the noon meal. She hurried to his side.

"Is there anything here to read?" he demanded brusquely.

"No," she replied.

The next day, the scene was repeated—the same question, the same answer.

"If you don't get me something to read I'll go out of my mind!" her husband finally shouted. Rosa was frightened.

"I have a confession to make," she said timidly after a few moments. "One day, a man, a colporteur from the Bible Society, came by selling Bibles and I bought one, but fearing you would throw it away, I hid it. I can get it for you if you want to read it."

"Bring it here. I'll read anything!" the man shouted.

So, for the next few days, Rosa's husband quietly read the Bible, inserting bits of paper between certain pages.

One day, much to Rosa's surprise, he called her again.

"If what this book says is true," he said, "we are going to hell! We have to find out where we can get a Douay version of the Bible and compare it. Where can we get one?"

"I'm not sure," Rosa replied, "but when I was growing up I lived near an evangelical church and the people there all had Bibles. Perhaps that church would have a Douay version."

When Rosa arrived at the church, the custodian welcomed her.

"My husband is looking for a Douay version of the Bible," she said, indicating the verses he wanted to compare. "Do you have a Douay Bible here?"

The man's face brightened.

"One time, a missionary, Fred Smith, was here and left a Douay version," he responded. "Fred

Smith said that some day someone might want to look up those very verses and make just such a comparison."

Rosa could hardly believe her ears. She took the Bible back to her husband. Together they looked up the passages he had marked off. As Rosa read each one from the Douay version, her husband exclaimed, "It's the same . . . it's the same . . . it's the same!" Finally he said, "It is true! We must get someone to come and explain it to us."

Rosa's next trip into town took her back to the evangelical church. This time the pastor was there. He agreed to visit Rosa and her husband.

They were both converted and when a visiting evangelist came for special meetings, they were baptized. Their whole family was added to the church.

I knew all five of the Christians in this story—the colporteur who left the Bible at Rosa's house, the custodian who met her at the church, the missionary Fred Smith who "knew" someone would one day want that Douay Bible, the pastor who led Rosa and her husband to Christ and the evangelist who baptized them.

God literally had the right person in the right place at the right time in each instance. The apostle Paul noted something similar:

> *"I planted the seed, Apollos watered it,*
> *but God made it grow. . . .*
> *For we are God's fellow workers."*
> 1 Corinthians 3:6, 9

# MY TURN

## GERMANY, Europe————————

### Rosalie Flickinger

January 15, Friday. Mother died today. Four days ago I was with her. Now I am alone, an ocean away. God, why did it have to be this way? We prayed for You to take her before I had to leave. Wasn't it her wish, too?

Was it only three days ago we boarded the plane for our next overseas term? Even the ice storm which caused us to miss our connecting flight in Chicago made me think You were delaying me. But You waited until it was too late. You waited until the cost was beyond what I can bear.

She really is gone. Memories. Memories. Memories. Mother, how I loved you! I counted the days we were home, a total of 159, many of them at your bedside. What a gift! But why couldn't it have been just four more, Lord?

She was 89 and longed to be in heaven with Dad and with You. But Lord, this time the cost is too high; You've asked more than I am willing to give. I already gave up my new house and a lot of stuff. That was okay. I could handle that. But not this—not missing my mother's funeral. I need to say this final goodbye with my family. It isn't fair. Tonight I feel no comfort, no peace, no serenity,

no sense of Your presence. I know You are here,
but I don't feel it.

I received the fax at 4:30 p.m. telling of
Mother's peaceful homegoing. The moment is forever etched in my mind. My mind was already in
a whirl because of having a houseguest for the
week. *God, I have enough problems,* I thought. Here
we are housesitting because our apartment was
sold, and the housesitting includes the care of the
16-year-old daughter of the house. We're back
with no permanent place to live and not even the
prospect of one. I can't even weep alone. I have to
do it with strangers around, while trying to con-
centrate on preparing dinner for everyone. What
was it we ate tonight anyway?

January 16, Saturday. The sun is shining. I slept
well after having a good cleansing, healing "weep"
last night. This morning I finished reading
Madeleine L'Engle's *Two-Part Invention.* She tells
of her marriage to Hugh—and his death. She
often asked, "My God, my God, why have You
forsaken me?" She says it is okay to ask why.
Some of Mom's last words to me were, "I once
read that we must never ask 'why.' " Same problem, two perspectives.

Madeleine, you've got a point; it is alright to
ask why. But we can't do it forever. We must also
accept what God gives us. That was definitely
Mom's theology and so easy for her to accept. At
one point in Hugh's illness, L'Engle wrote, "I am
beyond anger, I am in a dark place where I simply
exist in the pain of this moment. It's too much.
It's not fair. It's statistically excessive." I'm not
sure what she meant by "statistically excessive,"

but I can't count the times I have said "it isn't fair" in the last 24 hours. I still don't understand the timing, but the bitterness is ebbing.

This afternoon we drove into the wooded hills. It was sunny and surprisingly warm for a January day. We walked deep into the forest to one of our favorite spots. I sat at an old rustic table, reading, thinking, remembering.

Mom always went outside to work in the garden whenever any of us children left after being home for a weekend or holiday. She said she couldn't stand to stay inside the house alone so she went out to commune with nature. Today I know how she felt, except that I didn't leave her—she left me! What a shock! I had no idea how alone you feel when you realize your mother has left you. As usual, she was right; there is something therapeutic about God's nature when you are lonely.

January 17, Sunday. We went to our English-speaking church as I could not endure the thought of going to our German church where I would not be comforted in my own language. Earlier this morning I read in my *Joy and Strength* devotional book the Scripture reading in Ezekiel 14:23: "Ye shall know that I have not done without cause all that I have done, . . . saith the Lord GOD" (KJV).

The author writes: "Joy is the lesson set for some, / For others pain best teacher is; / We know not which for us shall come, / But both are Heaven's high ministries." Lord, what is it You want me to learn?

January 18, Monday. Mom's funeral day. I could not go to work today. We drove to the mountains. *Perhaps they can help bring some comfort on this difficult day,* I thought. Dad's favorite psalm came to mind: "I will lift up mine eyes unto the hills, from whence cometh my help. My help cometh from the LORD" (Psalm 121:1-2, KJV).

I'm still not completely at peace about not having gone home for the funeral. I do hope I will get over this resentment about having to miss this day of togetherness with the family. I feel left out. I'm not a part of the natural bonding which takes place among siblings after both parents die. Being with my family means so much to me. Too much?

On our way home we stopped in Bern, thinking we could meditate in the beautiful cathedral. It was locked. As we walked away, the cathedral bells were tolling. It was 5 o'clock, which meant it was 10 o'clock in Kansas and time for the funeral procession. I thought, *What am I doing walking the streets of Bern, Switzerland, while my mother's funeral procession is in progress? It is like a bad dream. I missed the train somewhere. I'm not where I'm supposed to be.*

Later, we stopped at a roadside restaurant for a bite to eat. We couldn't even find a quiet gasthaus open. I was eating goulash soup when it hit me: *I'm eating soup while my mother's funeral service is going on! Have I no respect?* The soup stuck in my throat, tears welled up.

I can't even cry during my mother's funeral service without all these strangers watching and wondering what's wrong with this woman. I should at least be at home, but I have no home. Our suitcases are stacked in the corner of someone else's home. A teenager is there. It is her home; we are the intruders, and a houseguest is there for the week. Lord, missing my own mother's funeral and not even having my own private place to grieve and weep is more than I can bear today.

The family telephone call tonight reported a beautiful service. Many wonderful tributes paid, mother deserving them all. Too bad we didn't write them before she died. We need to give tributes to people before they die, when we can see the look on their faces in response to some kind words. Now it's done. She's buried. It's over. Maybe I can let go of it all and get on with life.

January 21, Thursday. Today when I prayed it hit me—I don't need to pray for Mom anymore! Made me weep all over again.

January 26, Tuesday. Read Job 38-42 this morning. God answers Job's questions. In plain words, God says, "Who are you to question what I do?" Job replies in chapter 42, "I know that you can do all things; no plan of yours can be thwarted. You asked, 'Who is this that obscures my counsel without knowledge?' Surely I spoke of things I did not understand, things too wonderful for me to know" (42:2-3).

Lord, I still don't understand the timing in this and very likely never will. But I know You are sovereign. You see the entire framework of my life. Right now I am only seeing a very tiny part of it and that part is crying out that You asked too much! Someday I may understand the "things too wonderful for me to know." For now, I can only agree with the psalmist: You can do whatever pleases You! "Our God is in heaven; he does whatever pleases him" (Psalm 115:3).

It has been several months since I wrote these journal entries. My hope is that what is most personal to me will be most useful to you. Henry Nouwen, writing in the preface of *With Open Hands,* said, "But aren't my own experiences so personal that they might just as well remain hidden? Or could it be that what is most personal for me, what rings in the depths of my own being, also has meaning for others? Ultimately, I believe that what is most personal is also most universal."

Over these months I have struggled deeply with the "why" of God's timing of my mother's death. I realized I could not accept what God gives as easily as my mother could in her simple faith and trust. I went through a period of intense anger toward the inscrutable character of God—a natural tendency in the grieving process according to the Old Testament prophets and Psalms.

As I read again in Job 42, I experienced along with Job his response to God in verses 4-6: "You said, 'Listen now, and I will speak; I will question you, and you shall answer me.' My ears had heard of you but now my eyes have seen you. Therefore I despise myself and repent in dust and ashes."

My eyes were opened when I came face to face with Christ and His suffering for me. Then I could truly let go and say, "Yes, Lord, after what You suffered for me, this is nothing. I will rejoice in being a partaker of Your suffering!"

> Dear friends, do not be surprised at the painful trial you are suffering, as though something strange were happening to you. But rejoice that you participate in the suffer-

ings of Christ, so that you may be overjoyed
when his glory is revealed. (1 Peter 4:12-13)

In *Joy and Strength*, Henry Scott Holland writes:

It is a tremendous moment when first one is
called upon to join the great army of those
who suffer. That vast world of love and pain
opens suddenly to admit us one by one
within its fortress. We are afraid to enter
into the land, yet you will, I know, feel how
high is the call. It is as a trumpet speaking to
us, that cries aloud, "It is your turn—endure. Play your part."

This was my turn. I played my part, but I did
not play it well. I can still remember when I almost felt my mother admonishing me for how I
was feeling and acting! It was as if she were saying, "Quit acting like such a child. This is part of
life. Take what God gives and learn the lessons He
wants you to learn."

Forgive me, Lord, for feeling the cost was too
great. The cost is nothing compared to Your love
for me—You gave Your life. I've only given material things—a dream house, security, stability,
time with family, memories. Do with me as You
please for I know Your love transcends anything I
can imagine.

The struggle is over. Thank you, Lord, for giving
me my turn.

*"[Y]ou will know that I have done nothing . . . without
cause, declares the Sovereign LORD."*
Ezekiel 14:23

# WE'LL BE BACK

## THAILAND, Southeast Asia

### Glenn Lewis

**P**iang Jai was our *ahma*. She did the cooking, cleaning and taking care of the children while Shelia and I studied the Thai language and planted a church.

Piang Jai lived in Udorn, a fairly modern city of about 100,000 people in northeast Thailand. She and her husband attended the struggling church we were trying to see to maturity. Every Saturday, Piang Jai, her husband and family would drive with us about 40 minutes outside the city to her village. After eating lunch with some of her extended family and friends, we would discuss Buddhism and Christianity.

It was on one of these trips that Piang Jai introduced me to the principal of the village elementary school. He was an older man who had been teaching for about 40 years.

Over the next few months, Satien, the assistant pastor of our church and I developed a good relationship with this man. We called him Crew Yai, which literally means "big teacher," but is also translated "principal."

It was a Wednesday afternoon when Satien and I went to see Crew Yai for the first time. We had been invited. However, we weren't sure that the invitation was serious or just offered for etiquette's sake. We climbed into my old Toyota pickup and headed out.

"What do you think, Satien," I asked. "Does he really want us to visit or is he just being polite?"

"I'm not sure," Satien replied. "Most folks like talking to *falangs* (foreigners)."

"Any chance he'd listen to the gospel?" I continued.

"Well, he's older and sometimes older folks aren't so willing to change what they believe. But he should be fun to talk to."

Crew Yai lived on a dirt road—mostly mud during the wet season, mostly dust during the dry season. Although Crew Yai had a house near the school in the village, he lived in this little bamboo hut on that dirt road.

"Anybody home?" I called as we got out of the car. At first there was no answer, but after Satien called, Crew Yai came out. He looked genuinely happy to see us, invited us in and offered us some cold water. The water in Thailand is always suspect, but it was hot and I was thirsty, so I drank while we talked.

"How long have you been here in Chiang Yeun?" I asked.

"Forty years," he replied, smiling, "ever since I graduated from teachers' college."

"You know a lot about this area, then?"

"I should!"

I liked his sense of humor and I liked his ever-present smile. In his 60 some years, he'd seen and experienced things I couldn't even imagine. So, before we left, I asked Crew Yai if he could teach me about the history of Thailand and specifically this area. He seemed surprised at the request but said he would be glad to do it. I told him I would return the following week.

"Well, what do you think, Satien?" I asked as we climbed into the truck.

"I don't know if he will ever open up to the gospel, but I think we've made a friend," Satien replied.

The next Wednesday we were back at Crew Yai's house. Both Satien and I sat and listened as he explained the rich history of Thailand. The first lesson lasted about an hour.

For several months after that Satien and I returned almost every week to discover more about Thailand and how it got to be the way it was. But one can't talk about Thailand without talking about Buddhism. After all, 95 percent of the Thai are Buddhist. In fact, the Thai enjoy talking about religion, so it was natural for our conversations to turn to what the Thai believe and specifically what Crew Yai believed.

I began to bring my Thai Bible with me and we started to spend as much time talking about Jesus as we did about Thailand.

Finally, on one of our visits, the subject turned to Crew Yai's need for a Savior. All the merit he had made as a Buddhist was not enough to get him out from under the burden of Karma, the wheel of life that, according to Buddhism, keeps a person from reaching freedom and ultimately what we would call heaven.

"Crew Yai," I finally asked, "would you like to have Jesus as your Savior?"

He looked at me, cocked his head to one side and nodded affirmatively.

Realizing I didn't have my Bible with me, I excused myself. "I want you to know that what I am telling you are the words of Jesus, not my words," I said as I went out to the truck.

*I can't believe it!* I muttered to myself. The Bible wasn't in the truck! There was always a Bible in the truck!

"I want you to read God's book for yourself," I said, apologizing for forgetting my Bible. "I'll be back tomorrow to show you how you can know Jesus." Crew Yai said he would be there.

Satien and I were encouraged. Not many people come to Christ in Thailand, but here was a man who was about to become a Christian even though he had been a Buddhist for over 60 years.

We returned the next day, but Crew Yai wasn't there. We went the day after. Still no Crew Yai. We asked around the village. No one had seen him. Had he changed his mind? Was he avoiding us? We continued to visit the village each weekend, but we never could find him. And over the next few months, every time we passed by, we stopped. Crew Yai was never home.

About six months later, Piang Jai found out that Crew Yai was staying with some of his family right in Udorn. She suggested I go see him right away because he was sick and not expected to live.

I found his house and knocked on the door. "He's in here," his niece said as she led me into a small bedroom.

I was shocked at Crew Yai's appearance. He was thin to begin with, but now he looked like he weighed no more than 80 pounds. He was also in a coma, his breathing labored.

Around his neck a chain held a half dozen Buddhist amulets. His wrists had been wrapped in string by Buddhist monks and witch doctors to ward off evil spirits.

I sat down on the edge of his bed. Why hadn't I prayed with him without the Bible? How could I have forgotten it? Why hadn't I been able to find him? I prayed that God would give me one more chance. Just one more chance.

But Crew Yai didn't wake up. I never saw him alive again.

*"For God, who said, 'Let light shine out of darkness,' made his light shine in our hearts to give us the light of the knowledge of the glory of God in the face of Christ. But we have this treasure in jars of clay to show that this all-surpassing power is from God and not from us. We are hard pressed on every side, but not crushed; perplexed, but not in despair; persecuted, but not abandoned; struck down, but not destroyed."*
2 Corinthians 4:6-9

# ADIOS!

## COLOMBIA, SOUTH AMERICA————

### Helen Constance

It was time for the disassembling of another cherished home. Boxes of things for national pastors and barrels to be sent to the States occupied the dismantled living room.

In the dining room, red earthen pots of African violets with hundreds of blooms splashed their vivid colors. And along the high partition that separated our home from the adjoining one, pots of begonias lined the whitewashed wall with red and white blossoms.

Our children's bedrooms, along with their prized possessions, were taken apart with the painful thought that never again would things be the same. Colombian living for us was over.

I cried as I worked. God had called me to be a missionary before I met my equally called husband. And I loved my work. Now, he was needed in America for a very important ministry. So why couldn't I swing into the new situation with joyful enthusiasm? Though I couldn't sing through the gloom, I felt His presence.

Our three children left for school in Quito, Ecuador. We all knew that would be our last separation as a missionary family in Colombia.

After busy days, as George slept, I often sat in the darkness in our open patio contemplating the stars and praying. The violets and begonias gleamed in waxy beauty in the moonlight. They seemed to be the only living things that for a few more days belonged to us. Their profusion of blooms seemed to whisper that they cared about our leaving.

The city of Cali had tested our ability to survive in bumper-to-bumper traffic where everyone leaned on the horn, screamed at each other and defied traffic lights. George's travels away from Cali meant I had to pick up people at airports, bus stations and trains.

At first, I refused to take the responsibility, but George just looked over my head and beyond my fears and left anyway. It was up to me to learn to be as aggressive as the rest. So I honked and our fenders were bent like everyone else's.

There were unpaved, potholed back streets where the poor in tiny houses eeked out a living and barefooted children swarmed in the sunshine. The influx of people fleeing the horrors of war created slums with unbelievably terrible living conditions. People desperately hunted jobs that did not exist—at least for them. In the age of electricity, women still washed clothes on cement slabs in rich homes, happy to be servants for a pittance.

But Cali also had quiet streets with flowing bushes and beautiful shrubs, streets where the bougainvillea's graceful branches fell like fountains over the walls. These suburbs gleamed with bright tile roofs and wide avenues. Professionals parked late-model cars in the driveways of their mansions. As we made last visits to friends and churches, we knew that part of us would be left in Colombia.

Oh, how we had grown since becoming missionaries! We had stumbled our way into the hearts of patient people who loved us in spite of botching their beautiful language and holding on to "ridiculous" American customs.

We had been humiliated by fanatics and condemned by priests who preached evil things about us and accused us of being Communists. Through it all we had experienced God's working in our hearts in surprising ways.

I had followed my determined husband with a fearful heart, only to see the Lord surprise us with miracles. I had argued against new ventures, then stepped out on faith and went along, thrilled to see people come to Christ as I obeyed the Lord.

We had become parents of three beautiful children and these gifts from God enabled us to be one with hurting parents around us. Though we ached for our children far away in boarding school, we saw God fill the gap as we cared for others' children as He took care of ours.

Sometimes I grumbled that I was too tired to go on, only to find that as I repented I moved closer to Christ in an intimate and special way.

The last services in the Cali church were emotion-filled. Saying goodbye to the girls of my Sunday school class left my blouse wet with tears. The hugs of those who had come to know the Lord in that church, as well as those who came as refugees, sent us home that last night with the feeling of being loved and needed.

George and I thanked God for each other and that our love had grown year by year. Our divergent personalities had sometimes clashed, but the oil of the Spirit made our lives run smoothly.

During our final days in Cali, we went to the Andean "Hill of the Three Crosses" for the last time. As darkness fell, we watched the lights of the city blink to life, glowing golden in the night.

We stood embraced beneath the starlight, rejoicing that our love for Christ and for each other had brought unity of purpose, joy in living and sweet and satisfying human love. We knew God had brought us together and was ever there to smooth out the kinks through His patience and wisdom.

Our hearts grieved at the uprooting of our plans and leaving the Colombian people we loved. But we held hands and again stepped out in faith, thankful to do it together—with God.

*"Therefore go and make disciples of all nations. . . .*
*And surely I am with you always,*
*to the very end of the age."*
Matthew 28:19-20